THE DIANE MODAHL STORY

The Diane Modahl Story

Going the Distance

Diane Modahl

Hodder & Stoughton

First published in Great Britain 1995

British Library Cataloguing in Publication Data
A record for this book is available from the British Library

ISBN 0 340 64269 6

Typeset by Hewer Text Composition Services, Edinburgh
Printed and bound in Great Britain by
Mackays of Chatham plc

Hodder and Stoughton Ltd,
A Division of Hodder Headline PLC
338 Euston Road
London NW1 3BH

Contents

Acknowledgements

This book was written at a time when my husband and I were experiencing what then felt like our darkest hours. During our frustrations and battles throughout this ordeal my main motivation for writing this book was simply to use the opportunity to tell the *truth*, as it *really* happened. The book is not intended to harm, nor is it written with malice. Instead it is a true reflection of my life and events as I saw them.

Since winning the Appeal people have asked me if I feel bitter as a result of everything that has happened. Well, as painful as it has been, my faith and belief in God has made me into the person I am. I am not bitter, but angry that thirteen months of my life were a closed chapter and my future, our futures were in the hands of strangers.

I will for ever be thankful to my assembled medical team of experts: Professor Howard Jacobs, Dr Malcolm Brown, Professor Robert Owen, Professor Simon Gaskell, Professor Paul Talalay, Dr John Honour, Professor Rodney Bilton and Dr Reuben Gruneberg. All of them worked with dedication and commitment, often to the point of sacrificing time with their families – which applies to the *whole* team.

I do not know where to begin in order to express my thanks and gratitude to my legal team: Tony Morton-Hooper, a partner at Mischon De Reya, assisted by James Hardy, and instructed for the Appeal were Edwin Glasgow QC and Vincent Nelson. Their professionalism, unselfish dedication, commitment and motivation, despite the difficulty of having to deal with unco-operative and less than frank organisations was superb. *I have heard it said that a team is only as good as its leader and this I believe to be true in our situation. Tony and James left no stone unturned.*

I would also like to thank the many members of the public who sent me letters, faxes and postcards of support, whose encouragement made a big difference in my fight to clear my name.

I now turn to my husband, whom I have described as my rock of Gibraltar: my strength, pillar of support and most importantly a friend during my most desperate and lonely times during this nightmare. Vicente has backed me and passionately, to the detriment of his own health and personal development. This despite the fact that his own business and integrity was being questioned – he was also branded 'guilty' simply by association. Anybody who knows him knows this is simply not true.

To have Vicente by my side has been the most tremendous support I could have had. I love him dearly.

Diane Modahl
August 1995

Chapter 1

'Cover Your Face'

The Air Canada flight from Vancouver headed home to England. I was sitting in an aisle seat next to a stranger. Across the gangway from me was a nurse and beside her another athlete, Paul Edwards, muffled in a blanket. We were a party of three but each of us endured the long hours of early morning alone, preferring the company of our own thoughts.

Our seats were in business class, chosen as a deliberate precaution against anyone recognising me. I stared ahead into thin air, hardly noticing my surroundings. Other passengers were watching the film or listening to music on their headphones. I didn't even attempt to taste the food the air hostess brought round. I was locked in my own world where sounds couldn't pierce the cold silence and life went on in slow motion.

There had been so many flights before this one. (As an international athlete, flying to me was like hopping on a bus is for other people.) I remembered my first ever flight as an excited teenager, coming into land in Jamaica. From my window seat I could see the lights of Kingston shimmering below like the illuminations that held me mesmerised on childhood holidays at Blackpool. Years later, returning from the 1990 Commonwealth Games, I'd sat on another plane, taking my gold medal out of my bag time and again to hold it and convince myself that it was real. When we arrived at Manchester Airport that day, Paula Thomas, Ann Williams and I had made a pact to wear our medals round our necks as we walked off the plane. There was a small crowd of reporters waiting on the tarmac and we posed with our arms round each other. Nobody needed to tell us to smile. Like most athletes I was proud to have represented my country and to have stood on the winners' podium while 'Land of Hope and Glory' was played. I remembered performing a victory lap on the Auckland track, waving a Union Jack to the cheering crowd.

But this time and this flight were different. I was coming home in circumstances I could hardly believe: accused of dragging my country's flag in the mud. It was 24 August 1994, and I had been sent home from the Commonwealth Games in Canada. They told me a dope test I'd taken over two months previously in Portugal had tested positive for testosterone. To be told you've failed a drugs test is the worst news any athlete can hear, but to receive such a bombshell when you know it isn't possible, when you know beyond any shadow of a doubt that *you've never in your life* touched any banned substance, pitched me into an unreal world where right had become wrong and all sense had disappeared. To say I was stunned and distressed was a shallow description. When the news came it had sent me into such a state of shock that I still couldn't remember exactly what happened next. I'd broken down and reality had blurred into a series of nightmarish scenes which I tried to block out of my mind. A doctor had been called to sedate me before I was sent home.

The plane was banking. Soon we would be coming in to land at Heathrow Airport. My thoughts travelled back again to Victoria, to the stadium which should have seen me defend and retain my Commonwealth Games title. I was the favourite, I knew I had the fastest time and could win. By now the race would be over. There would be no gold medal, no glory, no lap of honour. I had been robbed even before I'd set foot inside the stadium. My name would have been withdrawn at the third call, only thirty minutes before the start. The English team management had assured me that the drug allegations would be kept from the press. They told me that it would be given out that I had a stomach bug. I hoped the security held; I was in no state of mind to face a barrage of questions and cameras – I had already been through the worst ordeal of my life and I didn't know how much more I could take. There was only one thing I kept at the front of my mind: the prospect of seeing my husband Vicente again. I desperately needed to feel the protection of his arms around me. In the sea of pain and confusion, his love was the only rock I could cling to.

The wheels touched the runway, bringing me back to the present with a jolt. Other passengers started to disembark. We waited to the last. The other athlete, Paul Edwards, had come straight from a Canadian hospital and had to be taken off the plane by stretcher. (I later learnt he was sent home because he'd failed a drugs test at the European Championships.) As we waited, I noticed four or five of the airport security guards had come on board and were hovering around us. I paced up and down the aisle impatiently. The other passengers were leaving the plane and I was anxious to do the same. There was a lot of whispering going on. The guards were discussing with the nurse how they were going to get Edwards off on a stretcher. I caught some of the words: 'The press are on the tarmac . . .'

I froze inside. What were the press doing there? How did they know so soon? I didn't know what to expect but I wasn't prepared for this. In Vancouver everything had happened so quickly once the decision was made to send me home. I'd been given no choice, I was placed on a conveyor belt and it took me away. They had promised no one would know the reason we were being sent home, there would be no reporters, questions or prying cameras. But that was in Canada, this was London the following morning and we were two English athletes.

The security guards were communing with their walkie-talkies. There was a lot of argument and confusion as we waited to be told when we could get off. Paul Edwards was getting agitated with the situation. 'How did the press get on to the tarmac?' he demanded. 'This is private property.' One of the security guards answered casually, 'Oh, they have special passes.' There was no escape – out of a window I could see lines of photographers stretching right out into the airport concourse. It was obvious they hadn't come because two athletes had been sent home ill. The scent of another drugs scandal in sport had reached them. The story was out – despite any reassurances I'd been given in Victoria.

The security staff were trying to find another route off the plane. In the end they decided that, while the other passengers went through the main concourse, we would exit by the back steps. A lift usually used for catering equipment could be employed to lower the stretcher down to the ground and get Paul Edwards into the ambulance. I would then follow the same route.

Edwards was lifted on to the stretcher, wrapped in a blanket and strapped on. As he was lifted out of the plane, he had the blanket pulled over him from head to foot, to hide his face from the press. Looking out of the open doorway, I could see the ambulance waiting on the tarmac and, to the right of the lift, a group of reporters with cameras poised. I was next. Seeing the press waiting eagerly below, I felt like a scrap about to be thrown to a hungry pack of dogs.

One of the security guards spoke before I stepped out of the plane. 'You might want to cover your face, love.' I swung round to look at him as if I'd just been insulted. Cover my face? I'd done nothing wrong! I wasn't ashamed. I would walk out on my own two feet and let them see me. I didn't intend to hide my head under a blanket like some guilty criminal leaving court. Mentally I was exhausted, bruised and shell shocked, but I hadn't forgotten the one thing that mattered – *I was innocent* and nobody was going to persuade me to act otherwise. To this day I don't know who that security guard was, he may have meant well, but he got my message and backed off, muttering something that might have been an apology.

I stepped on to the lift. The nurse followed me and we both grabbed the rail as the lift shuddered into life and began to lower us down. The only sound in the ghostly early morning air was of cameras clicking below. If the press had organised my arrival themselves, they couldn't have planned it better. There was no alternative but to stand there, pinned to that slow-moving lift, while the photographers had a field day. For the next few days, wherever I went, I was haunted by my own image on every front page and TV news bulletin. The pictures showed me leaving the plane in my yellow jumper, one hand in pocket, the other on the lift hand rail for support. My head drooped and my eyes were shielded by dark glasses. I looked bewildered, lonely and traumatised – which was pretty much how I felt inside. The lift reached the ground and we got into the ambulance. Once we were all inside, the doors slammed, the dark windows shutting out the world again. My long, arduous journey home was nearly over. But the living nightmare of the days, weeks and months ahead had only just begun.

How did it ever happen? How did I come to that day in August 1994 when my life was torn apart and my world shattered? My life up to that point gave me no hint of warning. I had parents who gave me a strong religious upbringing and wrapped me in the warm cocoon of a close-knit family. My childhood was full of happy memories. One of the earliest was the heady excitement I felt running alongside my sisters and my Dad in makeshift races he organised over the local fields. Later, when I grew up to become an international athlete, both my parents supported me with fierce pride in my career, keeping my scrapbooks and polishing my growing collection of cups and medals.

In Vicente I had a devoted husband; the day I stood at the altar rail beside him was the happiest day of my life. It was his coaching (building on the work of my first coach, Norman Poole) that helped me mature into a world-class athlete. I was Britain's leading 800 metres runner, the Commonwealth Champion, and had proved I was a contender for higher honours by coming fourth in the 1993 World Championships. The following year was all set to be the peak of my athletics career – until that day in August when I was stunned to find myself the focus of probably the biggest controversy that British athletics has ever known. The papers referred to it as 'The Modahl Affair', but what about the person who lived and breathed at the centre of it? No one knew how she felt. No one understood her pain or anger. From the first day I was accused, I kept silent and let others speak for me. I had my reasons – one of them being survival.

Yet throughout my ordeal I knew that one day the time would come to tell my own story. Not the one that was told in the papers, nor the one that was told by the host of commentators, coaches and athletes who lined up to give an opinion on my case, certainly not the one-sided version told by the BAF and IAAF who chose to believe in my guilt. This is my story, told in the hope that what I went through will never happen to any innocent athlete again.

Chapter 2

Early Steps

It was the year that England won the World Cup. Geoff Hurst, Nobby Stiles and all were parading round Wembley with their socks down, kissing the little gold trophy, but I missed the fun, for the simple reason that 1966 was the year I was born. My Mum and Dad were living in a red brick terrace in Raby Street, a row of council houses in the Moss Side district of Manchester.

I come from a large family – seven children – and I was the baby of the tribe. When I was born on 17 June, there were already four girls in the house: Doreen (5), Caroline (3), and the twins Debra and Barbara, who were 2. My two older brothers, Clive and Howard, were still out in Jamaica waiting to come and join us on the day there was room in our crowded house. I'm told my sisters weren't too thrilled to see the newborn baby – they resented having their Mum taken away from them for over a week. The day she walked back through the front door, clutching a tiny bundle to her chest, they were naturally suspicious.

My Dad, Sydney Edwards, made the trip from Jamaica in 1960. He came alone, promising to send for my mother when he'd sorted out a job and a place to live. Initially he stayed in Moss Side where his uncle owned a terraced house which acted as a temporary address for any relatives who made the long trip from the West Indies. When my mother, Lena, arrived a year later, my parents lived in one attic room overlooking Alexander Park where they went for Sunday strolls to breathe the air and admire the flowers. In those days Moss Side was a very different kind of place; you could leave your milk and bread on the doorstep all morning and it would still be there when you came home.

Eventually Dad got a job at Wall's, making up the pastry for pork pies, sausage rolls and pasties. He had to drive quite a distance to work and got up early, around five in the morning, to leave the house. By the time we children woke up my Dad was always gone. When he came home in the evening, we always had to say 'Good evening, Dad', and if we didn't there would be trouble. When it came to discipline and manners he was as strict as most Jamaican fathers; we children learned to respect our parents. We would all say our 'Good evening' very quickly to get it over with and then disappear off into another room, pretending to have important homework to do. We knew we had to be quick or Dad would enlist us on one of his 'fixing and trixing' jobs and we'd be lumbered with holding the torch in the freezing cold while he tinkered with the engine of our ageing Morris Minor van. He was always mending something – the stereo, the speakers, the van – or hammering something into a wall.

My Dad had two other great passions in life: music and watching televised sport. He couldn't live without his music. On a Sunday he would have it turned up loud, booming out of the speakers – reggae, calypso or a Ray Charles record that he'd recently found in a shop somewhere. There was always music in our house; Aunt Vera used to send us tapes from Jamaica with all the family news and what the brothers at church were doing. At the end of the tape we knew she would burst into song, one of the high-pitched religious songs they were singing at church at the time. Then she'd sign off with a last message: 'We've still got the pigs and it's raining.'

Dad later fixed it so he could hear his music all over the house, speakers running into the kitchen, speakers in the bathroom so you could sing along in the tub, even wires running down into the cellar where he kept his fish tank, his budgies and all the tools he hoarded for doing odd jobs.

Sport was his other great passion. One of my earliest memories is watching the Saturday afternoon television with my Dad. He worked the early morning shift on a Saturday and at mid-day we would meet him in town with my Mum. We waited at the same shop every week, then we all set off to the market in Longsight. My Dad's job was to help carry the bags full of rice, potatoes, cauliflower and broccoli. Once home, he'd unload the shopping, then settle down into his armchair in front of the TV to pick his horses for the afternoon. Saturday afternoon sport on television

was a ritual as predictable in our family as the great family lunches
that my Mum cooked on Sunday.

It wasn't just racing, any televised sport was an exciting event.
In our house you didn't just watch, you took part. If it was boxing
or wrestling my Dad would be shouting and yelling at the screen:
'Lick 'im, punch 'im! Go for it, you can win, man!' If it was
wrestling my Mum was just as likely to be there too, screaming
at Big Daddy, 'He's behind you, look out! Come on, come on!' I
remember staring at them as if they were mad sometimes, because
they obviously weren't affecting what was happening on the TV
screen. But soon I learned to join in with my older brothers and
sisters; if all nine of us were watching there'd be bedlam in the
front room.

The best time of all was when the athletics season came
round. We found ourselves watching black people taking part
and winning. In those days we very rarely saw images of people
from our culture at all, the quiz shows, comedies and dramas
were all played out in a world that was totally white. In athletics
we were seeing black people in a positive light and we'd always
scream and shout for them to win. If it was the Commonwealth
Games or the Olympics with a Jamaican athlete taking part, Dad
would call us in and we would all cheer them on like crazy to the
finishing line, jumping up and down and yelling encouragement
at the screen. If it wasn't Jamaica, we didn't care who it was –
black or white, Kenyan or British, if we saw someone who was
tiring coming into the final bend, we'd shout, 'Come on, keep
going, you can do it!'

There was one athlete who made an impression on me above
all others; he was Mirus Yifter, the legendary Ethiopian distance
runner. He was so majestic that he almost seemed to be playing
with the other athletes in a race. He would sit in the pack for
most of the race and then kick with about a lap to go, and when
I say kick, I mean he left the others behind as if they were
sleepwalking. Yifter was superb. Those Saturday afternoons in
front of the television were my first taste of the atmosphere and
excitement of international athletics. I can't remember ever saying
I was going to be like Mirus Yifter but the runners on the screen
had captured my young imagination.

The house we moved to when I was a few years old is the
one that holds all my childhood memories: 12 Bryant Close in

Longsight was a council house on the corner of a quiet cul-de-sac. It had three bedrooms and somehow we packed in my parents, my four sisters and two brothers who by that point had joined us from Jamaica. Clive and Howard had their own room, Mum and Dad had their bedroom and we five girls shared the other one. It was a bit like sardines in a tin but at that age I happily accepted things the way they were. The twins had a bunk bed whilst I shared a double bed with my older sisters Doreen and Caroline, them at one end and me avoiding their feet at the other. It was a small house considering the bodies we crammed into it, but cosy and always clean, a typical Jamaican house. Downstairs were the living room, dining room and kitchen and each of them was crammed with ornaments, pictures and mementos. Every inch of window sill or shelf was occupied by an ornament, coloured glass fish being a special favourite. Above them pictures vied for space on every wall – photos of the family, especially my grandparents, uncles and aunts back in Jamaica. My family have always been devout Christians, so pictures of the Virgin Mary and the Last Supper took pride of place. Sport came a close second, represented by a photo of Muhammad Ali, the World Heavyweight Boxing Champion and one of my Dad's heroes.

The dining room was for visitors and children weren't allowed in; my Mum always kept it spotlessly clean. The kitchen and living room were the rooms where we ate, talked, argued, watched TV and played our games. I would never say we were poor, but looking back on those early days in Longsight it can't have been easy for my Mum and Dad, both of them out to work and seven children to feed. Money wasn't readily available and we certainly had to be careful. I never got everything I wanted but there were always Christmas presents, meals on the table and a new school uniform when we needed one. New clothes were something we treasured, they were kept only for Sunday school, which was a special occasion. Some of our friends wore their new clothes as soon as they got them; we didn't, they were far too precious for everyday wear.

My twin sisters and I would sometimes dress up in my mother's old clothes, clip-clopping around the house in the high heels, bell bottoms or mini skirts which were in fashion at the time. Mum was a nurse; she set off to work at Withington Hospital around eight in the evening to work the night shift and returned to make our breakfast next morning. Then she would get us ready, see us off to school and probably collapse in bed for a sleep. With Dad setting off to work in the early hours, it meant my oldest sister Doreen was sometimes a second mum to us young ones. I liked seeing my mother in her smart nurse's uniform with the starched white cap. Around my tenth birthday I remember getting a nursing outfit with a little medical kit bag and for a long time I was determined to be a nurse. I was fascinated by my Mum's work and used to ask her all kinds of questions about what she'd done that day. I was especially interested in her stories about dead people and the way that sometimes when she closed their eyes the lids would slide open again.

When she wasn't at work my mother spent a lot of time in the kitchen baking cakes which she might put away for Christmas or give to a friend or neighbour. I was allowed to take part in the stirring and mixing and licking of spoons afterwards, although it was only Doreen and Caroline that really did much of the cooking. Food has always played an important part in Jamaican culture and in my parents' house Sunday dinner remains the big event of the week to this day. I don't think it has changed that much since we were seven hungry kids sitting round the table waiting for the steaming dishes to come out of the oven.

These days on a Sunday you can still find me and my husband Vicente, along with several of my sisters and brothers and their own children, round at my parents for the evening dinner ritual. Vicente and I arrive about 4.00 pm to be greeted by the sound of Dad's reggae thumping out from the living room and two or three nephews and nieces who run up and hug us around the knees. We go into the living room and have a chat with Dad or browse through the Sunday papers while the music is playing. Someone will start setting the table and gradually we'll all drift into the kitchen, drawn by delicious smells. Mum will have been cooking since the morning and food suddenly starts to appear like magic – from the oven, from pots on the cooker or from bowls in the fridge. A heady mixture of smells fill the air. A mountain of roast potatoes, browned rice with kidney beans, jerked pork (pork marinated overnight in a traditional Jamaican spicy sauce), chicken, gravy, carrots, broccoli or cauliflower – the table is covered in hot steaming dishes. We all pitch in and help ourselves as the talk gets into gear. We laugh loudly, crack jokes at each other's expense and sometimes get very heated about athletics, religion, Doreen's singing career (she used to sing with Simply Red) or whatever is happening. If someone has finished eating it's their turn to get up and let someone else sit down – there are never enough chairs to go round – they simply move to the back row and carry on talking. It says something about my parents and the close-knit family I grew up in that, twenty years on, most of us are still round there on a Sunday. My mother has never hesitated to welcome any boyfriends or girlfriends even though it means two sittings for dinner. I think it has helped to keep our family together; we all get on well and it shows on a Sunday.

These days the dinners take place at my parents' five-bedroom house in Withington. It was a big step from the council houses at Longsight where I grew up. There were no big gardens at Bryant Close so we were used to playing with the neighbouring kids out on the street.

The games we anticipated most eagerly were the races my Dad organised for the kids in our neighbourhood. He would arrive home from work at Wall's in Glossop and ask, 'Do you want to go running on the fields today?' to which there was always a chorus of 'Great! Brilliant! Fantastic!' from us children. On the way to the nearby fields, he would knock on the neighbouring doors and start rounding up our friends to make up the numbers for the races. The posse of my brothers and sisters all took part so by the time we arrived there was often quite a crowd. Dad must have looked a bit like the Pied Piper as he led a swarm of eager, excited children along Bryant Close to the fields behind.

When we arrived he would begin to organise all kinds of relays, sprints and team games. The longest race of all was always saved to last – a run to touch the telegraph pole and back, a distance of maybe 100 metres or more, which to my little legs seemed like running a mile. Dad would group us in ages, the twins would run with me and he would be running alongside too. The final race stands out in my memory because it held a prize for the winner – Turkish Delight that was conjured from inside a brown paper bag. It was in big, pink jelly chunks covered in chocolate which I would always lick off the outside first. Sometimes there were ice-creams too; on one occasion my Dad had to go back to the house for more money because there were so many children taking part. It wasn't only the winners who got a prize but my Dad will proudly tell you that I often won my race, even though I was by far the youngest. Who knows what part Turkish Delight played in deciding my later career? It was certainly my first experience of competitive sports which I have never forgotten. Even though I was exhausted by the end, I wanted to go on running more and more races.

I was about 7 years old when I had my first experience of living away from home. It happened because of a children's game that went too far. I'd been away from Longsight before but only on day trips – our annual holiday to Blackpool where we all climbed in my Dad's patched up old van (an embarrassment to us all in our teenage years) and drove to the seaside.

On this occasion it started with a visit from my Uncle Mel in Gainsborough, who'd brought my cousins to stay. Coming from Lincolnshire they spoke with an accent that seemed very strange to us but we had a lot of fun playing together. The day they were due to go home, one of my younger cousins, Sharon, said to me, 'Why don't you ask your Mum if you can come with us?'

'She'll never let me go, I've got school next week,' I told her.

My cousins weren't so easily put off: why didn't I hide in the back of the car and they could take me home without anyone knowing? I was the youngest and the most impressionable so I went along with the idea. Long before my cousins were due to leave I got in the car and they put a blanket over me. There were a lot of other bags in the back so I was concealed by luggage. I hid there for what seemed ages before I heard my three cousins getting in and everybody shouting goodbye. Then the door closed, the engine started and the car started to move off. Not surprisingly with a 7-year-old stowaway in the back, there was a lot of giggling from my cousins. Once, my Uncle Mel asked, 'What's all the laughter about?' but he kept on driving. After a while it got very hot and stuffy under the blanket. I was uncomfortable with my cousins squashed against me, so I got up. My uncle looked round in astonishment.

'What are you doing here?'

We were just approaching the turning to the motorway. 'Okay, do you want to stay or do you want to go back home?' he asked.

'I don't know,' I answered truthfully. I'd never been in this position before.

'Say you want to stay, say you want to stay!' Sharon whispered to me.

'You'll have to tell me now or else I'll be on the motorway and I won't be able to turn back,' said my uncle.

In the end we carried on and the decision was made for me. My uncle must have telephoned my Mum at a service station or when we got to Gainsborough. I don't know what she said but she wasn't at all worried about me staying. I was there for what seemed quite a long time, I even went to school with my cousins. Perhaps some parents would have jumped in the car immediately to bring their youngest child back, but Jamaican family life was different. In my parents' culture it wasn't unusual to hand a child over to grandparents, uncles or aunts to look after. One of my brothers, Howard, had stayed with my uncle in Gainsborough when he first came from Jamaica, so it wasn't a big issue for me to stay there. The extended family is a much closer thing in Jamaica than it is in Britain.

I enjoyed my stay in Gainsborough. They had two rabbits in the back garden, a park nearby and a typewriter that I used to play with. I don't remember saying, 'I want to go home', I was quite happy in the big house with three bedrooms and a garden. In reality I may only have been there a week, but to me it seemed a long long time.

Back home I returned to my Church of England primary school in Longsight. We used to have religious assemblies where we sang a lot – no hardship for me since music was a natural part of my life at home and at church. The highlight of school, however, was the Sports Day. I was already familiar with my Dad's races over the fields, so I looked forward to the egg and spoon, bean bag and wheel barrow races. My parents would usually be there watching and cheering us on. I can't say I stood out as an international athlete of the future at that stage but I think I won the three-legged race a couple of times!

Every Sunday we went to church. Religion was always present in my childhood, from the pictures of the Virgin Mary on the walls to the familiar sound of Aunt Vera singing spirituals on the tapes she sent from Jamaica. We children attended Sunday school at Brunswick Parish Church. I liked going; we did the usual things, such as listening to stories and painting pictures of Noah's Ark.

In the evening we went to Brooks Bar Pentecostal Church which was a different atmosphere altogether from C of E. Like all our neighbours we would dress up for Sundays in our best clothes. Arriving at the door we'd greet other families, the grown ups looking immaculate in their hats, best suits or dresses, with a Bible or a tambourine tucked under one arm. Once the service began, formality was thrown to the winds. There was a lot of singing, clapping and shouts of 'Hallelujah!' People stood up from their chairs to throw their arms in the air to praise God. As a young child I found it exciting, wild and loud, sometimes a little scary when the Holy Spirit entered into one of the congregation and they started to shake and speak in tongues. I knew it was a special language you could use in prayer but to an 8-year-old it was still a bit spooky and I would move in to sit as close to my mother as possible.

There was always a lot of singing, which was the part I liked best. Sometimes someone would spontaneously break into the opening line of a hymn and then the whole congregation knew it immediately and took it up. You could sing out at the top of your voice and really enjoy praising God. At the end of the song we would pray. These prayers weren't led from the front, everyone prayed out loud at once which gave the effect of a low mumbling going on all around the church. As a young girl, I used to stand there pretending to pray, but with one eye open watching the adults because I didn't really know what was going on.

After prayers, the choir would burst into song, which was a sound to shake the rafters. There was a great rhythm pounding through the clapping and the tambourines, the choir would sway from side to side, not just singing but giving their heart and soul to praising the Lord. The preacher might then ask if anyone wanted to come up to confess their sins and be forgiven. People would go up and kneel down as the preacher passed along the line and prayed for them. I didn't often get out of my seat but occasionally Mum would say, 'Just go up and get prayed for.' Reluctantly I'd have to begin the long walk to the front with the others. At that age I was a bit in awe because I knew what was coming. The preacher wouldn't just mumble a prayer over me, when he reached me his hand would clamp my head and he'd thunder in a voice to wake the dead. I would be so relieved when he'd finished and I could walk back to my place and sit with my Mum again.

As my brothers got older and reached teenage years they stopped attending church but my sisters and I kept going. When I was young I'd gone because my parents told me to but later I made my own choice to attend another Pentecostal church. Years after, when I was married, I took my husband along to one of the churches we used to attend when I was young. It was important to me that he experienced the type of church that I'd grown up in. Vicente is a Catholic so it was quite different from the kind of service he was used to but he enjoyed it. He thought it was more like a night out where you could talk about everything and nothing and sing at the top of your voice. There was no one saying, 'Now turn to page 55 and we'll say so and so.' It was spontaneous.

My parents didn't bring us up to fear God in the sense that we felt condemned for life if we didn't go to church. I thought of God as kind and loving. The mental picture I had of him was an old white man with long hair who was listening whenever you prayed and would answer. That was the image of God the pictures around the house had shown me and the one I'd seen in the epic film *The Ten Commandments*!

At home we said grace before meal times but otherwise family prayers were reserved for special occasions. In my early teenage years when I first started running cross-country, my mother would always say, 'God go with you' as I left the house for another race. My faith has always been important to me and I've grown up to trust in God first and foremost and believe that he won't give you anything bigger than he thinks you can handle. Later in my life that faith was to be put to a harder test than I could ever have dreamed possible.

Growing up in Withington near Manchester in the 1970s, I attended a multicultural school. There were plenty of other black girls of my age so I can't remember my race ever being a point of issue. It was at Ducie High Secondary School that my talent for running first started to show itself. I didn't excel at school academically but I could run. I couldn't throw the javelin, jump hurdles or throw the discus, I could run. Cross-country, rounders, track events – I was winning and it was fun.

Ducie High had a headteacher, Mr Blackwell, who was probably one of the greatest influences on my early development. He would always ask how my athletics was going and encourage me.

If there was a school sports event he would stay late to watch and often give me a lift home afterwards. In time he became a friend of the family and was later the master of ceremonies at my wedding.

My twin sisters Barbara and Deborah were also talented runners and used to stay behind with me for sports training. When I was 11 years old something happened one evening that lifted my running out of schools sports and gave me the chance to compete on a different level. It was the last training race of the evening, a 400 metre lap of the concrete track which had to double as the school car park. Deborah and I were running the race with some other girls near our age. Deborah was very tall and rangy, a good athlete who used to beat me most of the time. In this particular race my Dad was there watching so there was a lot of pride at stake. Coming into the last bend, Deborah and I were neck and neck, out in front of the others. Both of us were so eager to win we were straining every muscle and, as we reached the line, my sister stumbled and fell, grazing her knees badly on the concrete track. The race was a draw but I claimed victory because she fell!

We weren't aware that there was someone else watching that evening. Alan Robertshawe, a coach for Sale Harriers, was out talent spotting. After Deborah's wound had been cleaned up, he approached us and said, 'Well done, you both ran really well.' He asked us if we'd like to join a track club. We weren't entirely sure what that meant but we said yes anyway, probably because it was flattering to be picked out.

I didn't know it at the time, but in Sale Harriers I was joining one of the top running clubs in Britain. For many years it has been one of the top female clubs and has one of the biggest recruitment schemes for young runners in the country. The club has won numerous titles and honours and produced several athletes who have competed in the Olympics: Michelle Scutt, Kevin McKay and Andrew Ashurst among them. In 1994 Sale Harriers had six athletes at the Commonwealth Games and the club provided all three British women athletes competing in the 800 metres at the European Championships that year.

As a young girl joining my first track club, I wasn't dreaming I would ever compete in the Olympics. In those early days Sale Harriers was just good fun, it gave me a chance to make friends of my own age. Training wasn't particularly hard, it was geared to giving us a good all-round introduction to athletics. We were divided into groups of around twenty or more with arrivals starting in the blue group and progressing by age or talent to green, red, purple and orange groups. At the training ground at Crossford Bridge, we did long jump, high jump, hurdles (or tried to) and ran laps and laps of the Sale school playing field.

With both the twins and I running, it meant my parents had to find a lot of sports kit and footwear. They bought me what they could afford but there wasn't always money for all the latest gear. I used to get a lot of hand-me-downs from the twins, such as warm jumpers and tracksuits. A man called Mr Saunders who had two daughters at the club also used to give me a lot of their old kit. Running spikes were especially prized. I can remember waiting for Helen Saunders to finish a race so that her father could take the spikes off her feet and clean them up for me to wear in the next race. Mr Saunders always made sure the trainers or spikes were spotlessly clean before he passed them on to me; I didn't mind that they were second hand – I treasured them as if they were brand new.

It wasn't long before I was taking part in competitions. Sometimes it was a road race but more often cross-country. I have vivid memories of those races. Cross-country was muddy, freezing cold and always seemed a very long way to the finish. I still enjoyed it because it was running, but I don't remember volunteering to make up the numbers!

In one race during winter it was actually snowing heavily when we arrived. My mother had come to watch as Deborah and I were both racing. As we lined up at the start, we were frozen to the marrow, neither of us dared even think of taking off our tracksuit tops. As I stood next to her, I could see my sister was decidedly unimpressed by the whole idea. The gun went off and around two hundred runners headed off into the woods, splattering through the snow and heavy mud. The course was very hilly which didn't make things any easier. I soon lost sight of Deb as I battled on in the middle of the pack, slipping, climbing, twisting, trying to keep my footing in the slushy mud. It was one of the most awful races I can remember but I finished somewhere in the middle. I found my mother and asked her what had happened to Deb; it turned out she'd had enough and dropped out half way through.

After that day my mother used to give me a little glass bottle to take with me to my races. She used to say, 'Take a little sip of that before the race and it'll warm you up.' So I'd go off with my spikes, a warm jumper, a flask of hot Vimto and my little glass bottle. It was some time before I found out that what she was giving me was a tot of whisky to keep me warm. It's a story we've laughed about many times since.

As they moved into their late teens, my twin sisters started to train less and less often. They were two years older than me and there were other things on their minds – music, boys and late-night clubbing held a greater appeal than running in the mud and freezing cold. Unfortunately for them, the late nights weren't so easy to come by because of my Dad's strict ideas about discipline. He didn't mind my sisters going to night clubs as long as they came back at what he held to be a respectable hour. In practice this meant he would drop them off at the club about 8 pm when the doors were hardly open. (This, after they had spent about two hours getting ready, all four of them fighting for a turn to do their make-up in the bathroom!) He would then arrive at the club promptly at 10 pm to take them home again. As the youngest I went with him on these trips and sat waiting in the faithful old Morris Minor van outside (we still had the same one which my sisters loathed to be seen in). If they didn't appear at the time appointed, my Dad would determinedly head inside the night club to look for them. For a group of teenage girls trying to act cool with their boyfriends, it was a major embarrassment. They told me later that if one of them saw him coming they would run and hide so that they could hang around a little longer. I was luckier: by the time it was my turn to go out in the evenings, he'd eased off a little.

I was not one to get in trouble often. It may sound dull to some but I didn't swear or get in fights as a teenager. About the worst thing I did (which I don't think my mother knew) was to smoke a couple of times when I was about 17. The twins who lived across the road from us had become my close friends, their parents were quite wealthy and gave their daughters an awful lot of freedom compared to me. They were smoking like there was no tomorrow and persuaded me to try it.

We were brought up to respect our parents and to accept their authority. My mother will tell you I was the kind of child who couldn't tell a lie and hated to be in trouble. Once, when I was very young, I put a toy car's rubber wheel on my finger and couldn't get it off. Too scared to tell anyone for fear I'd get in trouble, I kept it on my finger all day. The finger started to swell up and turn blue because the wheel was stuck on so tight. I tried getting it off with soap and every way I could think of but without any success. It wasn't until dinner that evening that my mother asked, 'What's that on your finger?' My whole finger had gone black by then so I got in serious trouble anyway for not owning up! It's a trivial incident but it's one of the few times I can remember I was in trouble with my parents. Honesty, truthfulness and respect were ingrained in my childhood both at home and at church. I grew up to have faith in God, to trust in his will, and to believe that you could achieve things with your life if you worked hard and honestly.

I was committed and disciplined in my running from the start and it rapidly began to take up all my time. Belonging to Sale Harriers increased my self-esteem because we were very successful as a cross-country team. It gave me a great thrill to return home and show my Mum and Dad the trophies, seeing them mounting up week by week on the shelves. Three of us Edwards sisters ran for the club and we still have press cuttings from those days. At the age of 12 I saw my picture in a newspaper for the first time. It was the *Liverpool Echo* and their photographer snapped me in the last leg of a relay race in Sefton Park, coming in to finish in a pair of plastic trainers, a T-shirt and running shorts worn over my black tights. The caption said, 'Nothing can deter 12-year-old Diane Edwards, not even the biting cold.' I can still picture everyone looking at me and clapping as I was coming in. It was my first press cutting and I probably treasured it as much as any that came later.

As I got keener and stronger I started to catch up with my older sisters. This wasn't always popular and in at least one race it caused a problem. The occasion was a road race in which I competed with my sister Barbara. Over the three-mile course I had paced myself well and was catching Barbara, although she had started quite a distance ahead. Yet every time I tried to pass her she would snap, 'Get back! Get back!' I thought there must be something wrong and I'd drop back to run behind her for a while. Then I'd try again to overtake and she'd say, 'Your

breathing is putting me off. You're breathing heavily. Get back!'
So I'd drop back again, not knowing what to do. At last I decided
that if I ran past her really quickly she couldn't say anything.
I carried out my plan and, at the end of the race, finished in
front of her. It wasn't until years later that she confessed she
just didn't want to be beaten by me. That race brought me
my first prize, a little silver trophy that my mother still keeps
at her house.

By the age of 15 I was very committed to my running. I was
channelling all my energy and ambition into it. So much so that
when a chance came to visit Jamaica for a six-week holiday, I
insisted that the headteacher, Mr Blackwell, must guarantee that
I could keep up my training. I had my coach type out a training
programme so that I could run while everyone else was going on
the beach.

The majority of the children at Ducie High School had West
Indian families and Mr Blackwell wanted us to see Jamaica to
learn about our culture and meet the relatives we had never seen.
Naturally the idea was so popular that there was an overwhelming
number wanting to go. Not all of us could afford the fare but
our headteacher enterprisingly wrote to the Prince's Trust and
managed to get some funding. The trip was unique enough for
us to be accompanied by a TV documentary crew. They thought
the idea of second- or third-generation West Indian children seeing
their parents' or grandparents' birthplace for the first time would
make a fascinating programme.

In the end three of our family went on the trip: Barbara,
Caroline and myself. My Mum and Dad were delighted and
wrapped up a big parcel of gifts to take to our grandmothers
and other relatives. We spent the first half of our stay on the
university campus in Kingston. True to my word, I would get
up early each morning to run round the grounds. The island
was just the way my parents had described it, lush and green,
bananas growing on the trees and the occasional lizard basking
on a rock in the sun. I soon decided I could never live in Jamaica
because of the insects – I hated all the midges, moths and flies.
When we stayed out in the country, the three of us slept in one
bed with only a blanket to cover us. If I woke up during the
night I would watch in horror as the cockroaches marched along
the wall.

For the second half of the holiday our school party split up to see various relatives. My mother's mother lived in the very last house at the top of a steep hill in the countryside. I can picture the day we arrived laden with luggage and carefully wrapped gifts. We were expecting to be met by a donkey my mother had told us stories about. The donkey didn't make an appearance, there was only a sudden tropical downpour to greet us. In Jamaica, when it rains it really rains, the drops are warm on your skin but you get drenched if you stay outside. A lady who lived on the corner took pity on us and let us take shelter in her house.

The rain didn't look like stopping so we decided to climb the hill anyway. It was a gritty, sandy road and the stream of water running down was starting a minor landslide. When we finally scrambled to the top, still clutching our damp parcels, we were met by a small, sturdy old woman with short hair. Her face reminded me both of my own mother's and of my Uncle Mel in Gainsborough. My grandmother was so delighted to see us that she took us straight inside and insisted on washing our feet to get the grit off. When I think of her today I can still see her with a bowl of water, kneeling down to wash our feet.

She cooked in an outside kitchen. During our stay we ate huge meals of yams and ackee (rather like scrambled eggs), green bananas, salt fish or meat. Despite my training at Kingston University, I put on an enormous amount of weight. My grandmother was a very calm, deeply religious woman. Her conversation was peppered with Bible verses and she could recite long passages off by heart. Outside the house was a wide garden where she showed us the tomb of her husband and our grandfather, whom I sadly never knew.

It was a wonderful trip and one that stands out in my memories of adolescence. Yet I didn't find anything of myself in that country. I was glad to see all the places and people that my parents had grown up with and described to us a thousand times, but there was no direct connection with me. I belonged in Manchester with my family in our warm, crowded, cosy house in Raby Street. I belonged in Ducie High School and Sale Harriers where I had just begun to glimpse a future for myself in running. Yet I couldn't have dreamed that the next time I saw my grandmother I would be coming back to Jamaica as an Olympic athlete.

Chapter 3

On Track

Ambition wasn't something I lacked even at the age of 15. It may be a quality I get from my mother. She is never content to let life pass her by. She has a positive outlook and is determined to achieve things with her life. It is typical of her that at the age of 54 she decided she would learn to swim. We were on holiday in Jamaica at the time, and she learned in the sea with the help of Vicente's mother. But she wasn't content to leave it at that. When we returned home she secretly started going to the local swimming baths and took her width and length swimming certificates. She passed both first time. No one in the family knew anything about it until she came home one day proudly holding these proofs of her achievement. For someone from a background where money was scarce, my mother has always been ambitious and is always looking at courses to take or property ventures that she might invest in.

In that respect I'm like her, I have too much energy to sit around and let life pass by, there are lots of things I want to achieve. From the start I found an outlet for my ambition in running, and I channelled all my energy and commitment into that one goal. In my early career I'd have to admit my single-mindedness about athletics closed off other avenues in life to me. I was very selfish as an athlete, I would sacrifice almost anything to go training, and I would become almost unbearable if I had to miss a training session. Even at the age of 15 I was reluctant to go on the trip of a lifetime to Jamaica if it meant sacrificing my running for a few weeks.

Throughout my early teens I was competing in school championships, and with Sale Harriers, both in cross-country and track.

At Sale Harriers I was a member of many a winning team in local and national cross-country events. The highlight of my cross-country racing was the National Championships. There were five hundred girls running and I came seventh overall. It was also a great satisfaction to me that I came in ahead of Bernadette Eli, one of the top runners at Sale Harriers – although in fairness it has to be said that she got a piece of wood stuck on her spikes that day which may have slowed her down!

Running through the cold and mud was good training for my later career in international athletics; I gained stamina and determination – I never dropped out of a race no matter how awful the conditions. Yet I realised early on that if I had any ambition to be a top athlete, cross-country would have to take a lesser role while I focused on the track.

It was clear from the beginning that the 800 metres was going to be my event. Sale Harriers is known as a middle distance club and offers very good coaching at that level. I was never really quick enough for short sprints and had no talent for throwing, hurdling, or jumping, even though I tried them all. The coaches at Sale pushed me towards 800 metres because it was an event that suited my strength and stamina.

The 800 metres is an event that requires a range of disciplines. Although it's two laps of the track it's fast progressing to become a long sprint with the world record currently set at 1 minute 53.77 seconds by the Czech runner, Jarmila Kratochvilova. There are three main qualities needed to become a world class 800 metres athlete. You need the speed of the 400 metres runner for the first lap, then you need the speed endurance of the 1500 metres runner; finally on the home straight you need courage and determination to win the race. People often make the mistake of thinking it's the fastest runner who wins, but in the 800 metres it's the strongest runner. She is the one who is able to maintain the finishing pace approaching the line, when the other athletes are tired and slowing down.

The 800 metres swiftly became my event at school and I ran in four English Schools Championships. Three times I came second and on the final occasion, in July 1984 at Thurrock, with my family there to cheer me on, I won the race, breaking the English Schools record in 2 minutes 5.7 seconds, a time that still stands today. By that stage, I had already represented my country at several junior international events. The first was against France in Lille when I was 16. I was doubly excited to receive the letter because not only was it my first international, it was only my second trip on an airplane. Air travel became a way of life later but I still have the ticket for my trip to France.

The following year, 1984, was the Los Angeles Olympics and with it came a trio of important events in my life: my first job, my first Olympic trials and my first serious relationship.

The job was working at Ron Hill Sports in Hyde where I started in October 1984. Ron Hill is a famous name in sport to anyone who remembers Britain's greatest marathon runner, but today he is well known as the chairman of a sportswear and equipment company. My job was to take orders from retailers or wholesalers. Fortunately for me, the company secretary left soon after I joined. The managing director, Mike Deegan (another athlete), asked if anyone could type. I volunteered and started to type letters for him, eventually becoming his personal secretary. For my last two years I worked a three-day week to fit around my athletics. It was a job that suited me. I was a quiet, conscientious worker, and rather shy in those days. Ron Hill and Mike Deegan supported and encouraged me in my running and Ron was later able to advise me on altitude training in Mexico City, having run there in the 1968 Olympics.

In the summer of 1984 I had a late call-up for the Olympic trials at Crystal Palace. I was still only 18 and excited just to be involved. In the trial race I ran a new personal best time but it wasn't good enough to qualify for one of the places in the team.

While the British Olympic team – Sebastian Coe, Tessa Sanderson, Daley Thomson and co – were competing in Los Angeles, I was taking part in a slightly lower profile event, the Bell's Junior International in Edinburgh. It was a two-day meeting where I won my race, so I was feeling elated. After the competition we would rush back to our accommodation at the university to watch the Olympics on television. That was the year the Eastern Europeans boycotted the games, so we were seeing a lot of Westerners winning, names we hadn't seen before. The Americans were very dominant that year, virtually making a clean sweep in the sprint events, with Carl Lewis winning four gold medals. There were also British success stories to savour: Sebastian Coe, Steve Cram, Tessa Sanderson and Daley Thompson in the decathlon.

I remember vividly watching my event, the women's 800 metres, and thinking that I could have been there, lining up in the vast stadium watched by millions the world over. I wasn't disappointed or jealous, it was just exciting as a young junior athlete to have been so close to taking part in the greatest athletics event in the world. I can recall cheering on Lorraine Baker running a great race to come fifth behind Doina Melinte, who crossed the line to take the gold.

Next time, I said to myself, I want to be there.

Edinburgh was also the place where I had a near disaster and met my first serious boyfriend. The evening after I had won the 800 metres at the Bell's International, the organisers were holding a disco for the athletes as a celebration. The winner of the 400 metres that day was another English athlete, Derek Redmond, and part way through the evening he came over and asked me to dance. I had seen him on many occasions before because we were taking part in the same athletics meetings, but this was really the first time we had met.

Later we went out for a stroll together around the university campus. It was a warm midsummer evening and we stood on a bridge that looked out over the lake. Edinburgh was a beautiful place and we were two young athletes who'd just had a great day, with every reason to look forward to the future. One day we both aimed to be part of a British Olympic team ourselves, rather than watching it on television. We spent the rest of the evening together, walking and talking in the grounds. We discovered we had a lot in common, including our sense of humour. In fact we were enjoying each other's company so much that we completely lost track of the time.

The problem was that our team managers, Sue Deaves and Marea Hartman, had set an 11 pm curfew by which time all junior athletes had to be back in their rooms. This wasn't an unusual rule at a Junior International; athletes are like any other young people and likely to get up to all kinds of things away from home! When our team managers said be back by 11 pm we knew they meant exactly that, discipline was strict and anyone who broke the rules was asking for trouble. But Derek and I were so busy talking that we didn't notice we were past the curfew time until it was too late.

We said a hasty good night and I ran back to the accommodation. I got in about 11.30 pm and crept up to my room praying fervently not to be seen. Unfortunately I was sleeping next door to Marea Hartman and just as my hand touched the handle of my door, she came out of her room. Marea was one of the old school who ran her team of 'gels' like a boarding school headmistress.

'Oh, young *lady!*,' she thundered in a scandalised voice. 'What *have* you been up to? You'll never run for England again.'

I mumbled my apologies weakly. She replied that I should go to bed and the situation would have to be discussed in the morning.

As anyone can imagine, I went to bed but didn't get any sleep that night. I was a junior just starting out on my international career, winning races and with every chance of joining the senior ranks. Now my promising career appeared to be over before I'd even got started – and all because of a walk with another athlete in the university grounds. I wondered how I was going to explain all this to my mother. I could almost picture her shaking her head in disappointment. In the end, as the first light began to steal through the curtains, I decided that my only option was to go to Marea Hartman in the morning, tell her the whole truth and apologise.

I knocked on the door early, having rehearsed what I was going to say a hundred times in my head. Marea Hartman let me in. I said, 'I'm so sorry about last night. I did meet Derek Redmond and we were walking on the campus. We got carried away and we didn't realise what the time was. I'm really very sorry and it will never happen again.' How many times could I say sorry? I went on like this, apologising for all my life was worth.

Marea waited till my speech had tailed away, then said she was glad I was sorry. The incident would be forgotten, providing it never happened again. For all her strict classroom manner, I soon discovered that there was a soft centre to Marea Hartman.

I was able to laugh about my sleepless night later. It was so unjust – Derek had gone happily back to his room and never heard a word more about it. He was my first serious boyfriend. We had both gone out with other people before but we both realised this was something different. After Edinburgh we swapped addresses and, from then on, wrote to each other every day. He lived in Northampton and I was in Manchester so it wasn't too far to go and stay with each other's families for weekends. At the same time we were both progressing through the ranks together as athletes, more or less keeping pace, so we saw each other at international meetings. We went out together for two years and perhaps would have gone on longer if something hadn't come between us. He was the first person I told that I loved and I believe he felt the same way about me, but the relationship was sadly to be cut down in its prime.

The coach who worked with middle distance runners at Sale Harriers was Norman Poole. We trained at Stretford and he used to coach the whole group at that level, but with me, it soon became clear that he was prepared to invest more time and work than usual. He would pick me up and drop me off at races at weekends, buy me multivitamins, and do anything that would progress me as an athlete. He was always there, encouraging me at races or giving me advice by telephone if I was away on an international. For my part, if I was asked to take part in any race, no matter how prestigious, I would always ask Norman before committing myself; he was my coach and knew what was best for my development.

It was around this time, in 1983, that one of my sisters, Deborah, had a serious accident. She fell around twenty feet from a balcony window, breaking her back and suffering numerous other injuries. To add to our shock and distress, she was pregnant at the time (thankfully her little girl was later born safe and well).

Deborah was in hospital for a long time and in a lot of pain. In many ways I could see it was a desperately hard time for her. When she was alone and suffering she told me that her only source of strength was to pray. The God we had believed in as children, going to the Pentecostal church with our parents, had never disappeared from our lives, but now something new was happening – I could see he was changing my sister. Almost overnight she became a different person: open, honest, giving, and more likeable than ever. She was able to understand and answer questions from her own faith and experience. It was a change that's hard to describe without it sounding pious, but the same thing later happened to my brother Clive. It was obvious that somehow my sister had come closer to God and it had brought out a new depth in her.

When Deborah finally came out of hospital she again started

going to a church, this time one where a lot of younger people attended. I went along too because the change in my sister had also rekindled a flame that had dwindled in me. I had always continued to pray but now I began reading the Bible every day to look for answers about life.

At the Pentecostal church I started to attend they had a time of fasting every year. The idea was to go without food for a short period to focus on what mattered and draw closer to God. I was keen to do it like everybody else but when I spoke to my coach, Norman Poole, he argued strongly against it. He said it would have been an absolutely ridiculous thing for a serious athlete to consider, I wouldn't be able to train for a week or even longer because I'd be so tired. There was even the danger I might end up making myself ill. I don't think he realised how serious I was about fasting and how important my faith was to me then, but in the end I was persuaded to give up the idea.

Later on we had a similar argument over giving blood. I wanted to give blood because it was a way of giving something back to other people but again Norman was adamant that athletes don't give blood. He argued that I couldn't afford to do it, I might become anaemic and too ill to run. Again I gave in. Running was important to me and I didn't want to jeopardise my progress. After all, he was my coach and the man in the know, so if he said something wasn't a good thing then it couldn't be good.

In a way these were minor issues though important to me at the time. But in 1984, when I started to go out with Derek Redmond, it soon became clear that my coach felt this was another thing that would come between me and athletics. He would describe what we had as just a holiday romance. We didn't see each other every day, he pointed out, we were lucky to see each other at weekends, so of course it all seemed nice and exciting. Our relationship was based on an artificial situation where we only saw each other on rare occasions. It was the same story as before, when we'd disagreed over fasting and giving blood; he was trying to convince me that running and running only was important. Derek Redmond was only getting in the way. For a long time I refused to listen, serious doubts only crept in as I reached my twenties and my career started to take off. I saw then that I could potentially become a world class athlete – could I afford to gamble with that chance?

By 1985 I knew I was one of the British athletes being groomed for the next Olympics in Seoul in 1988. I was invited on a trip to South Korea, with the idea of seeing the new purpose-built stadium and adjusting to the long flight and change in time zone. We weren't actually allowed to race on the Olympic track as it was still being finished, but we raced in another stadium and I won in 2 minutes 5.7 seconds, beating a Japanese athlete and Susan Sirma (who later went on to win a silver medal at the Tokyo World Championships).

During the trip we were taken to see the Olympic stadium itself. For me it was like taking a small bite out of the future to savour the taste. There were workmen still hammering and working on the arena, but what arrested my attention were the rows upon rows of seats, hundreds and thousands stretching back up to the skyline. Sue Deaves, the British Women's team manager, stood with us and said, 'Take a good look – I hope some of you will be coming back here in three years' time.'

A determination hardened in me. 'I'm going to be one of them, I'm going to race on this track,' I said to myself. As the coach pulled away from the stadium, I took a long, last look back out of the window, fixing the place in my mind for when the time came.

Sue Deaves was to become a familiar figure in my life, accompanying me as team manager on trips from my junior days into the senior ranks. Hers is an immensely responsible job which takes in everything from registering athletes to sorting out who runs in which lane and who is rooming with who. Some officials were anonymous figures but with Sue I built up a personal friendship – there was always a nod or a wink to greet me. On tour, she was something of a mother figure for the female athletes, very understanding and experienced, always there if you needed someone to talk to. She has the gift to make you feel you can reach the goal you are striving for in athletics. Ironically, years later, it was her sad task to tell me the most devastating news I have ever been given in my life.

As I approached my twentieth birthday, two major events loomed large in my sights: the Commonwealth Games and the European Championships. Both were to be held in 1986, so that gave me a year to transform myself from a promising junior into someone who could be a serious medal contender. In the 1985 season I gained a lot of valuable experience running against some of the best 800 metres athletes in the world. My baptism on the Grand Prix circuit was at the Bislett Games in Oslo, Norway – it was a rude awakening for me and a race that I still cannot think of without a sense of embarrassment.

My invitation to take part resulted from a race in Gateshead where I came third in a very strong international field. Andy Norman, then promotions officer for the British Athletics Federation (BAF), approached me to ask if I'd like to race in Oslo. I was taken by surprise and unsure how to answer. I'd watched the Bislett Games on television and knew that it was a great honour to take part. I was worried that if I didn't say yes immediately I might miss my chance. On the other hand, if I agreed and my coach didn't want me to go, I'd have put myself in an awkward situation. Andy Norman was probably surprised I could hesitate at the Bislett Games but I told him that I'd have to talk to my coach first. He nodded. 'Just give me a ring tomorrow and let me know.'

Norman Poole readily agreed, the Bislett Games was a great occasion, it was too good an experience to miss. A short time later I found myself in Oslo with the cream of the world's 800 metres runners. Doina Melinte, the Olympic gold medallist, was there, along with Ana Quirot and Shireen Bailey, the English record holder. Shireen had been dominating British 800 metres running for some time and took me under her wing from the time we arrived, giving me a few useful words of advice.

The Norwegians love athletics and, as we came out on the track, there was a big crowd making a lot of noise. Lane eight seemed so close to the spectators that you could almost reach out and touch them. It was all just the way I'd imagined it. My first Grand Prix event on the surface known as the World Record Track. It is a fast track kept in superb condition with very little wind inside the stadium because of the surrounding city tower blocks. I knew Sebastian Coe, Steve Cram and David Moorcroft had all set world records on this track. And here was I, Diane Edwards from Sale, only 19 years old and racing against some of the best female 800 metres runners in the world. I was excited but not overawed, I knew that I was in good shape and I was prepared for anything – anything except what happened.

The gun fired and we went off with the pacemaker (a 400

metres hurdler) out in front. I tucked in behind her, in second place, thinking that everybody else was right on my tail too. I could hear the crowd roaring in my ears and they were yelling for me – the unknown English girl out in front. It was a fast time and they love that in Oslo. We went through the bell in under 56 seconds, which at the time was only a second slower than my personal best for 400 metres. It was just after the bell that I felt the first twinges of discomfort. I'd been relaxed and enjoying it but then it started to get hard. Going down the back straight for the final time, with 300 metres still to go, I suddenly came to a virtual stop. I felt like my legs had gone. The pacemaker had dropped out and a blur of coloured vests rushed swiftly past me. I could still hear the roar of the crowd but it was all in slow motion. My vision was gone, I could hardly move my legs and I suddenly felt very lonely. The other runners were so far off up the track I could no longer see them, only hear the cheering of the crowd as they neared the tape. I realised that I'd made a terrible mistake in running the first lap so fast.

Then I gritted my teeth and said to myself, 'Come on, you must keep going, don't drop out, don't drop out.' I pumped my arms as well as I could and pushed myself on. I was probably jogging. As I finally lurched across the line I walked off and burst into tears. I'd never felt so humiliated in my life. There I was on national television, looking like I was going to win and set a world record time (I thought that all you had to do was set foot on this track and it would happen) and the race had ended in a complete disaster. I wanted the earth to open up under my feet and swallow me, so that I wouldn't have to face anyone.

But other people didn't see my performance that way. They kept coming up to me and saying, 'Well done, you ran well.' I didn't want to look them in the eye, I felt like apologising for just being there.

Back at the hotel, Andy Norman, the BAF promotions officer, also wanted to speak to me. Instead of criticising, he said, 'You ran really well. I'll reward you for that. Do you want to go to Larvik?'

Larvik I'd never heard of. 'Where's that? When is it?' I asked.

'Don't ask questions. Do you want to go or don't you?'

I hesitated again. 'Can't I just ring my coach and ask him?'

'All right,' he sighed, 'but I need an answer.'

I went off quickly and found a telephone to call Norman Poole. 'Did it look awful?' I asked. I had a tearful conversation but he consoled me by saying, 'Go to Larvik and run like the Diane Edwards you know. Go there and race.'

I went and ran well, finishing third in the race. But my first Bislett Games I will never forget. It was a shattering introduction to the very highest level of athletics. You could call it my baptism of fire. Oslo seems to be a place where things happen in my life, because a few years later when I took part in the Bislett Games I met my future husband. Unknown to me he had also been there in 1985 as a pacemaker in the steeplechase. By the time we met, five years after, a lot had changed for both of us.

This was also the year I got my first full international vest for Great Britain. The occasion was East Germany versus Great Britain. We all got new kit for the competition which would have been exciting if the kit hadn't been so horribly old-fashioned – long pointed collars and flared tracksuit trousers. Coming from the junior events like the Bell's International where it was all fun, everyone seemed to take it all very seriously at senior level. It was a nerve-racking occasion but I ran well, coming third in the 800 metres behind the two East Germans who were later to take gold and silver at the next Olympics.

The year had finished well and when 1986 dawned I was in confident mood. It was my year of opportunity with both the Commonwealth Games and the European Championships taking place. It was to be a good year for me, apart from the one sadness that I split up with my boyfriend, Derek Redmond. We'd been seeing each other at weekends and international events whenever possible but all the time I was hearing the voice of my coach at the back of my mind, telling me this was an unnecessary obstacle to my progress.

I was still a vulnerable and impressionable 20-year-old. I thought that if I didn't listen to my coach I might never make it right to the top. One weekend, when Derek had come to stay at my parents' house, I told him that we had to stop seeing each other. I said that it wouldn't really work – which, sadly, wasn't what I truly felt. The split was just as painful for me as it was for him and I think I regretted ending the relationship almost immediately. It was hard for Derek to understand my decision at the time, but today it's all in the past and I'm glad that he's happily married. As for me, I was to wait another four years before I found someone else I really cared for.

I'd be the first to admit that I owed an awful lot to Norman Poole's coaching in the first half of my career. But there was a downside. Problems arose as soon as anything conflicted with his control, where he couldn't have an influence. If I started to think for myself or to make my own decisions then he would soon attempt to put a stop to it. Of course someone might argue that he was doing only what was best for my athletics career and I certainly didn't question anything my coach said or did then. Things were shaping well for me. At the age of 20 I'd made the transition from junior international to running against world-class athletes and, after a bumpy start at Oslo, had by no means been disgraced. Yet I had still to win a medal at a major championship. The Edinburgh Commonwealth Games represented my best chance. That season I was running consistently and winning against some strong fields; others had started to notice that I was a strong contender for the gold medal. I was well aware there was no shortage of competition, not least from Kirsty Wade, the Welsh girl who had won almost everything that year. I knew I'd have to run the race of my life to beat her.

While I was in Edinburgh preparing for the Games, I got a call from my Dad. My mother was away visiting her family in Jamaica but he suggested coming to watch the final. From Manchester, it was so close he could be there in a few hours. I told him, trying to sound casual, that I knew exactly what I was doing and that I'd be fine, he shouldn't bother. My family hadn't come to see me run that often and I was worried it would put a lot of extra pressure on me if they suddenly turned up for a big occasion like this. It was left that he wouldn't be coming.

I qualified for the finals easily and felt relaxed and confident when the big day arrived. I lined up with the other athletes and, when the gun fired, set off sharply. We had only reached the 50 metre mark when I heard someone in the stand screaming, 'Go on Diane!' I recognised my Dad's voice immediately. In fact he had ignored our telephone conversation and was there with two of my brothers and sisters, all yelling at the top of their voices. I tried to put them to the back of my mind and concentrate on the race.

The first 100 metres had gone well and I was in a good position but then things started to go wrong tactically. The other runners started to come around me and I slowly found myself being pushed towards the back of the pack. It was a physical race with a lot of runners bunched together closely and several times it looked certain that someone would fall. Coming into the home straight for the first lap I was still well back and could find no way through on the inside. I did the only thing I could which was to slow down to a jog and drop right to the back. Then I accelerated up the outside going all the way round. I passed the other runners and reached the front just behind Kirsty Wade who was leading comfortably. Tactically, it was something you should never do because a sudden surge uses up precious energy which needs to be kept in reserve for the final 100 metres. When we rounded the final bend I was still on Kirsty's shoulder and knew I was in with a chance. As we came to the line it was very close, there was only a vest between us, but I had already spent my last ounce of strength and had nothing left for a final burst. Kirsty Wade took the gold, breaking the Commonwealth Record. I had won a silver medal.

It was my first medal at a major games and, though I felt disappointed at missing gold, I enjoyed my moment on the rostrum. I had seen other athletes win medals on television and when it finally happened to me I thought I'd really arrived. It wasn't until the following year that I realised that silver meant nothing. You had to be a winner before people really started to sit up and pay any attention.

Chapter 4

Striking Gold

At the age of 20 I had my first medal to frame and hang on my wall. I could think back to all those afternoons as a child watching the athletics with my Dad, urging on the runners in the final straight. I wondered then how it felt to be one of the chosen three on the winner's rostrum, dipping their heads to receive their medals and waving to the crowd. It had finally happened to me. All those years of hard training, running through the cold and mud in winter had paid off.

I could have sat back and congratulated myself, but I wasn't content. I knew I still had a long way to go. I was a medallist at the Commonwealth Games but on the European and World circuit I was still just an also-ran. World-class 800 metres athletes were breaking two minutes consistently; I had yet to break through that crucial barrier. There were still two or three more rungs for me to climb to reach the highest level of middle-distance running. I was still only 20, time was on my side, and I believed I could get there. Whenever I was out training, the goal at the back of my mind was to reach the final of one of the big three – the Olympics, European or World Championships. The inspiration and effort were there; it was only a matter of time.

My next chance came with the 1986 European Championships in Stuttgart. After my Commonwealth silver I expected to be selected but it was still exciting to open the letter that confirmed I was going. In the event I ran my heat from the front and stayed there, winning it easily. But the next day I drew the harder semi-final against some of the best Eastern bloc runners and got knocked out. I ran a personal best time of two minutes flat but the first four places were run in under two minutes.

I had the frustration of sitting in the stand to watch the 800 metres final with my coach. I wanted to be out there on the track, warming up, feeling the nerves, stretching my muscles. I hated being a spectator watching with everyone else. I remember Norman Poole saying to me before the race began, 'Next time you're going to be there.'

A year later I found myself back in Oslo at the Bislett Games, on the same track where I'd felt so humiliated on my Grand Prix debut. Now I was one year older and more experienced, I knew I was much stronger both mentally and physically. I'd run in races of the highest calibre and I wasn't going to make the same mistake of thinking that I had only to set foot on the 'World Record Track' to run a fast time.

As usual it was a high-class field – Doina Melinte of Romania, Ana Quirot from Cuba and Sigrun Wodars. It was a big field so we started on the curve rather than in lanes. I was used to training like that in a big group bunched together so it wasn't something that bothered me. Again there was a pacemaker but this time I didn't make the mistake of going with her. I got away well and found myself in third place. Going down the back straight a gap opened up and I was aware that I was in front of some very good runners. I kept on the shoulder of Doina Melinte, the leader and was still there as we came round the final bend. Coming into the final straight I was aware of two girls on my shoulder and I knew it was down to who were the strongest finishers amongst the four of us. The other three were all world-class runners and when it came to the tape I was just a couple of metres behind. It seemed like another case of 'so nearly'. I walked over to lean on the fence where I could see my best friend and room-mate Paula Thomas waiting for me. I felt tired and desperately disappointed. She said, 'I think you've broken two minutes.' I shook my head. 'No, I ran rubbish. I thought I was going to win.'

'You ran really well, Di. I'm sure you've broken two minutes.'

Then I looked. There was the confirmation on the results board. 'Diane Edwards: 1 minute 59.30 seconds.'

I had broken the barrier of two minutes for the first time, on the same track that a year before had defeated me. Disappointment turned to elation. The signs were good. Anything under two minutes was regarded as a world-class time for 800 metres, so you could say that with that race I started to compete with the best. The goal that still remained was to reached the final of a major games.

The World Championships followed in Rome that year, 1987. Paula Thomas and I were both there, sharing a room as usual. Life was full and exciting. We were two giggling young girls, having fun, travelling to new places, supporting each other. At the most important times in my life Paula has always been there as someone to confide in. We were both progressing up the ladder at the same time, she in the 100 metres sprint and me in middle-distance running.

In Rome Paula reached the sprint finals, proving it was possible to compete with the world's best. I was not so successful in the 800 metres. Again I qualified easily for the semis but fell at the next hurdle. The Eastern Europeans were very strong and at that stage in my career I was having problems maintaining my strength from the bell to the point where there was half a lap to go. I broke two minutes for the second time but it wasn't enough, I finished sixth in my semi-final.

Just before the race I was in the changing room underneath the stadium. I heard a roar go up, it eventually died away and then gave way to an enormous cheer that must have lasted for ten seconds. I knew the men's 100 metres was taking place and I later found out that Ben Johnson had just broken the world record. Only one year later and his name was to make every front page headline for other reasons – as one of the first athletes to be stripped of a gold medal for drug taking.

Back home another record had been broken which was closer to my own interests. In 1987 Kirsty Wade smashed the British women's 800 metres record by two seconds, coming home in 1.57.42. It was a superb time and she was a competitor who was respected both in the UK and on the European circuit. There were other talented British runners around at the time – Shireen Bailey and Lorraine Baker to name just two – but Kirsty, who'd beaten me in the 1986 Commonwealth Games, was undoubtedly my main rival in Britain.

The winter season came with my sights fixed firmly on the goal of running for Britain in the Olympics the following year. My training was going to plan so there seemed no point in making any drastic changes. Then came a scare. During the early new year of 1988 I started to feel lethargic. Training sessions which normally weren't a problem left me feeling exhausted. I would set off running and after only a hundred metres start to feel shattered. At first my coach and I put it down to hard training but as the weeks turned into months and I showed no improvement, I feared something was wrong. In Olympic year any illness is worrying because every athlete knows it's vital to be in peak form for the season. There were only three 800 metres places in the British team and plenty of girls in the queue to fill them.

I went for numerous tests at the Alexander Hospital in Cheshire. At first my problem was thought to be a flu virus or glandular fever but ultimately it was diagnosed as toxoplasmosis, an infection picked up from a parasite. It is commonly picked up by eating meat that hasn't been thoroughly cooked or else salad or fresh fruit that hasn't been properly washed. I could only think I might have picked it up in a restaurant somewhere. The illness had been diagnosed late and I hadn't stopped training, so I may have made a quicker recovery than normal. I thought I'd put my problems behind me, but I was very wrong.

By spring, in the early season, I started to gear up my training to race speed. In May I took part in a Grand Prix race in Nice. I ran a shade under two minutes and felt in good shape. It was useful to get one good race under my belt and give an early reminder to the selectors of my form. I was the only British girl to have run under two minutes that season. It was a fact I was to be more grateful for than I realised at the time.

After the race in Nice I was back in training again. One day I was doing a session of 150 metres flat out. I'd started off at a terrific speed, giving it everything in the first ten metres, when I felt a sharp pain in my hamstring as I came off the bend. It was so severe I actually jumped in the air and pulled up. I could barely walk. As I limped away I thought, 'I've pulled my hamstring, this means no trials and no Seoul Olympics.' All the years of planning, working and hoping for my first chance to compete in an Olympic Games seemed to turn to ashes in that one unlucky moment. The trials were in June, the very next month, I could see no way back. I phoned my physiotherapist that night and explained what had happened. He advised me to keep the leg elevated and ice it every twenty minutes. Visiting him the next day there was good news and bad. I was relieved to hear it wasn't a severe hamstring pull, but the bad news followed – I wouldn't be able to run on it for weeks, which meant missing the Olympic trials.

I informed the selectors as soon as possible so that they were aware of my situation. There was still one road to the Olympics that was open to me. At the British trials, the first two across the line automatically get a place providing they make the qualifying time. The third place is in the hands of the selection committee. If an athlete is injured for the trials but will be fit for the Olympics, they can still be selected for the third place. For me it all came down to a simple equation: if nobody in the trials broke the sub two minute time I had set in Nice, then I was favourite to travel to Seoul as the third runner.

I went down to the trials to watch. It was nerve-racking, sitting there as the runners warmed up. There, looking tense, were the favourites, Kirsty Wade and Shireen Bailey, but in the pack alongside them were others such as Beverly Nicholson and Tonya McCulloch, hungry for their chance. Every athlete desperately wants to be in the Olympics, the chance only comes round once every four years. You will go out to train through rain or snow if it means getting there. I was gripping my seat nervously. I knew any one of these athletes was capable of producing an exceptional performance and dashing my hopes. It all came down to who ran best on the day. One race and the first two across the line. Then it was up to the selectors to decide the third.

It was a beautiful sunny day in Birmingham with spectators sitting on the grassy banks and filling the stands. The conditions were perfect for running. I held my breath as the gun went off. They set off fast and the first lap was run in under a minute; if they kept this up my time could certainly be beaten. Coming into the home straight I could see the front runners were giving everything. It was hard to know whether it was going to be a fast time or not. They took the tape with Shireen Bailey and Kirsty Wade in front. The time went up. It was outside two minutes. I jumped in the air, I knew I had made it. A couple of spectators sitting close by leaned over to say, 'Well done. You're in.' I was going to run in the Olympic Games for the first time in my life. It was difficult to really believe.

Once my place had been officially confirmed the next step was to collect the kit in London. Paula Thomas had been selected too for the 100 metres so I would have my best friend and room-mate with me. Athletes always get a fair amount of kit and freebies for international trips but we got our first hint that the Olympics is on another level when we opened the package. There were shoes, chocolate bars, teddy bears, jumpers, hats, caps, books and pins, not to mention the official uniform which was navy blue with a cream skirt. It felt like Christmas had come early. Ironically I never got to wear my uniform in the opening ceremony because we went to a training camp in Japan and had to miss the parade.

The idea of the Japan trip was to acclimatise for two or three weeks before the Olympics started. We were staying at a place called the Neon Centre alongside the Americans and a couple of other teams. It was a luxurious camp with superb facilities, including jacuzzis, massage rooms and saunas; or golf, badminton and table tennis if you wanted something more active.

There was only one thing to spoil the stay – my old friends the cockroaches, who had plagued my nights in Jamaica. We stayed in wooden chalets and in the warm weather they seemed to attract cockroaches like a breeding ground. Some of the beasts were up to three inches long with hard shiny backs. Four of us shared our bungalow: Paula and I in one room and Jenny Stoute and Simone Jacobs in another, but not one of us had what it takes to kill cockroaches. In the morning I would find them in my suitcase or crawling over the clothes I'd laid out for the day. Night time was worse – it was every woman for herself. The two rooms were separated by the kitchen and if Jenny or Simone came running out of their bedroom screaming, one of us would immediately get up and lock the door. 'Sorry, we can't help,' we said charitably. Hunting cockroaches in the dark was asking too much of friendship and, besides, we knew the next night they'd do the same to us!

This particular breed of Japanese cockroach was indestructible. Once, one of us threw a shoe at one on the kitchen floor and scored a direct hit. The thing was stunned but later when we came back it had gone on its way. A rumour went round that by keeping the air conditioning on you could keep the cockroaches away. Paula and I left ours on all day to make sure – when we came home later there were virtually icicles hanging off the ceiling. We tried another tactic: seeing some American male athletes passing one evening, we pleaded with them to come in our chalet and help us. They obliged, wanting to know what all the screaming was about. We pointed to a cockroach on the floor and demanded that they kill it. After they had whacked it about twenty times with a shoe the creature was still beetling around in dazed circles. Eventually they succeeded and, feeling they'd done their duty, went away, leaving the flattened ex-cockroach in the middle of our floor. None of us would move it, we just stepped over the corpse until the cleaning lady came the next day to take it away. I've run through snow and mud in the worst of conditions, with my fingers red and frozen to the bone, but ask me to pick up a dead cockroach and you're asking the impossible!

We left the Neon Centre without any regrets, said goodbye to the cockroaches and moved to the Olympic village. Before the Games started I relaxed by listening to music or watching TV. Some of us who were Christians, such as Kriss Akabusi, Loreen Hall, Vernon Samuels and myself, would sometimes meet to sit on the grass by the canteen to talk and sing a few songs of worship. We were out in the open air so other athletes from various countries – some Christians, some just curious – would sit down to talk or sing with us.

The men's 100 metres was run before my event and was won by Ben Johnson. I watched him win that race. Soon after the rumours started to go around the Olympic village that he had tested positive for drugs. Since I had first entered the international athletics scene there had always been stories around about athletes taking drugs. My event – the 800 metres – was dominated in the 1980s by the Eastern Europeans and it's now common knowledge that many of the athletes from those countries took drugs. We were aware that drugs were around in sport and I knew my event was one of the ones with a problem. But I never personally knew anyone who was taking drugs and if someone had suggested it to me I'd have wasted no time in telling them to get lost. My views on dope taking were well known – I wanted to be the best through my own talent and effort; anyone who cheated by resorting to performance-enhancing drugs, I viewed with contempt.

When the Ben Johnson story broke in the papers it didn't mean that much to me. I didn't know who this Canadian was other than that he was a great athlete. In a way the media frenzy started to overshadow the events happening on the track, which made me sad and angry. Paula Thomas and I were both due to compete the day the news became public. We were trying to ignore the uproar and focus on our own events.

When the 800 metres got underway I knew I faced three races in three days, providing I got through the qualifying rounds. In 1988 there was no rest day between the semi-final and the final. I arrived in Seoul placed no higher than 50th in the world rankings. My best time was 1.59.30 whilst some of the best athletes had run four or five seconds faster. Realistically my chances of making the final were paper thin, but that was the goal I set myself to achieve. I had never run in the final of a major games and there was no better occasion than the Olympics to change that.

A lot of good athletes were knocked out in the first or second round but when the semi-finals came I was still there. It was a warm afternoon and the full stadium was buzzing with anticipation as we came on to the track. Looking at the faces of the other runners, I knew the scale of the task I was facing. Christine Wachtel of the GDR, the American, Delisa Floyd, and Gaby Lesch of West Germany were all expected to make the final. Shireen Bailey had also been drawn in my heat. Of the eight British competitors taking their lanes, we knew only four of us would make the Olympic final. When I'd talked over the race with my coach, we'd agreed to treat this race as my 'final'. If I qualified it was a marvellous bonus, if not, at least I'd know I had given my best effort.

I was excited and nervous; you only got one chance in the Olympics and this was mine. The gun fired and when we broke lanes after 100 metres I was in a good position. Wachtel, Floyd and Gaby Lesch were all up the front, pushing the pace. As we reached the back straight for the final time, the leaders started to open up a gap, leaving me battling for fifth position with Lesch. The West German girl suddenly surged forward to close the gap with the front four. I knew if I wanted to stay in the Olympics it was now or never, and I went with her. As we came into the home straight it was clear that the first three places were decided, there was only one door left open to the final and either Lesch or I would go through it. We had been in tight finishes before and knew there was little to choose between us. I willed myself towards the finish, stride by stride inching ahead. As I crossed the line I threw my hands in the air. I'd finished in fourth place: a place in the final of the Olympic Games was mine.

It wasn't till after the semi-final that it hit me what I'd achieved. I remember being interviewed for ITV after the race. I was jubilant, on a high. I took the microphone and said, 'I've done my job. I came here to get into the final and I've made it, I'm really delighted.' It was my first major final and I'd done it at the Olympics. No one could have expected anything more of me. Neither Shireen Bailey or Kirsty Wade had qualified – I was the only one left to carry the flag for Great Britain.

The day of the final came and I went through the ritual all over again. A light jog in the morning, then trying to stay rested and relaxed. I was feeling confident and sure of myself. I even thought that I could win a medal. You tend to get ambitious when you've achieved something that you didn't really expect. I felt that the sky was the limit. I heard my name called out for the line-up, 'In Lane 1, Diane Edwards, Great Britain.' I put both arms in the air and waved to the crowd, turning to all four sides of the track. This was my moment and I was going to enjoy it. I wasn't the least bit nervous or overawed since I felt I'd already done my job. I was smiling and feeling good, there was no pressure on me at all. Mentally, I had already relaxed after the semi-final. But I was expecting to run just as well as I had done in the last two races.

The gun fired and the 1988 Olympic final was under way. The race set off at a tremendous speed but I was still in contact in about fourth or fifth position. Then gradually I became aware that the front runners were starting to pull away. I fought hard to keep in touch. It was not until the back straight on the final lap, where I'd had problems before, that the field began to pass me. I wasn't specifically trained to cope with the strength of that calibre of running. These were the elite of 800 metres runners in the world. As we came to the line I trailed in last in eighth place. My time was outside two minutes.

Again ITV wanted a post-race interview but this time they were talking to a completely different Diane Edwards from the previous day. I kept my eyes down and it was hard to get a word out of me. I was feeling total and utter disappointment.

'What are you going to do now, you've done your job, everything that was expected of you?' they asked.

'I suppose I'll just look around Seoul and enjoy the rest of the Olympics,' I said without much enthusiasm.

It was left to Paula Thomas to put the race in perspective for me. Later that day she said, 'Diane, you made the Olympic final. You were in the final eight. You made it, girl.'

She was right. I was 22 years old, it was my first Olympics and I'd been counted among the best eight female 800 metres runners in the entire world. The event was so dominated by the Eastern Europeans that I was one of only three Westerners who reached the women's 800 metres final that year. Only the finalists get an individual certificate to take home. I wanted to run the race all over again but in the end I was able to take a step back and enjoy what I'd achieved. I lived off that day for a long time. Seoul 1988 remains one of my best memories in athletics. There were so many moments to savour. Seeing Florence Griffiths – or Flo Jo as she was known – in full flight was one of them. She was American, a beautiful woman, a superb athlete and winning races, breaking the dominance of the Eastern Europeans. People said she did an awful lot to raise the profile of women's athletics that year. There were also high spots for the British: Liz McColgan winning a silver medal, Yvonne Murray a bronze medal, and Chris Cahill coming so close in the 1500 metres. Those performances convinced me that it was possible for athletes from 'little Britain' to compete on a world stage.

After my race was over I kept my word to see some of the sights in Seoul. One of the local market places soon got to know Paula and me among their best customers. All you had to do was jump in a taxi and mention the market's name for the driver to take off at great speed, zipping down narrow streets and through impossibly small gaps in the traffic. Taxi drivers have a reputation the world over but Seoul can boast some of the craziest.

Once at the market, it was possible to buy almost anything cheaply if you were willing to barter. There were shops on one side of the road and little street stalls on the other selling jewellery, socks, T-shirts, children's clothes and the inevitable array of Olympic memorabilia. Fake watches were being sold for £5 but if you bartered you could walk away with one for £2.50. Ten T-shirts could be bought for a pound. In the end Paula and I were going back almost every day to buy presents for my sisters and the rest of the family. She used to say, 'We can't buy anything else or there won't be room to take it all back.' The bartering was all part of the fun and we soon picked up the rules. The trick was to reach a certain point where, if you weren't willing to pay the asking price you'd say, 'I don't want it' and walk away. The stall owner would always come running after you calling, 'Missus, missus!'

The Games flew by and all too soon we were all gathered on the track for the closing ceremony. It was a very emotional event and will always be one of my lasting memories of the Seoul Olympics. Thousands of athletes from every nation under the sun – swimmers, boxers, runners, weight-lifters and gymnasts – were standing in the arena side by side. We had been asked to walk in an orderly fashion around the track but there was never much chance of that lasting long. We managed about 100 metres walking in our teams then everyone started to go wild, running in all directions. It's the moment when you release all the nervous energy that has been stored up over the past weeks. I had a pair of Mickey Mouse ears that I'd bought on a visit to Disneyworld whilst in Japan. I remember wearing these ridiculous ears while I ran around the stadium with another British girl, Loreen Hall.

At last we all calmed down and stood for the closing speech. There were thanks to all the competitors and officials, then the Head of the IOC said, 'This Olympic Games is now officially closed; we welcome the new Olympic Games in Barcelona in 1992.' There was a hush as we watched the Olympic flame die down. It had been my first taste of the greatest games in the world and for me it was a very emotional moment.

That year, 1988, will always rank as one of the best in my career. I had broken two minutes early on, winning the Nice Grand Prix, beating Slobodan Colovic from Yugoslavia and Kirsty Wade, the British record holder. To crown it all, I had reached an Olympic final, something that nobody expected of me before the Games began. At 22 I had established myself among the best 800 metres runners in the world. Yet I knew I could still get better. I hadn't run out of ambitions by any means – there was still the matter of winning my first gold medal. My thoughts were already travelling forward to Auckland in 1990 where the next Commonwealth Games would be held.

During the winter of 1989 I did a lot of indoor training with the aim of speeding up my preparations as the season was starting earlier than usual. New Zealand summer time dictated that the Commonwealth Games would be held in February. A week before the Auckland Games began there was a pre-Games meeting which gave me a chance to assess my chances. The field included most of the runners who would be contenders in the 800 metres. It was a 600 metres race and I was beaten into second place by the Australian, Sharon Stuart. Strangely enough, after that race I knew I could win the gold in the Commonwealth Games. In the 600 metres race I sat on the shoulder of Sharon Stuart and was unable to get past her. It made me realise that next time I would have to consider a different tactic. The obvious alternative was to take on the lead myself and dictate the race at my own pace, making sure that nobody came past me. It was a risk and right up to the moment before the gun fired for the Commonwealth Games final I was undecided which I should do. Should I let the Australian take the pace, let her do the work and attack later on, or should I take the initiative right from the start and make sure that no one could catch me?

Although there was that doubt in my mind, when the day came I felt so confident that I actually *knew* I would win. It wasn't a matter of arrogance; I'd trained and prepared well, I'd won everything up to that point in the domestic calendar and it was a field I knew I was capable of beating. Everything was in place for me to claim the first gold medal of my career. I could see it hanging there, waiting. But I wasn't going to fall into the trap of thinking it was a foregone conclusion. As we lined up for the final, I was aware that there were at least three other athletes who were capable of winning the race. Sharon Stuart was one and the two English girls, Lorraine Baker and Ann Williams, were also a danger. But I had to concentrate on my own race. There was still the tactical question at the back of my mind. Should I blast away right from the gun or hold back, waiting for the right moment? A race can be won or lost on a tactical error and my chances of Commonwealth gold depended on making the right choice.

The gun fired in my ears and I took off. Instinctively I knew then I was going to take the race on from the start. I went to the front, feeling relaxed and confident. Ann Williams was sitting on my shoulder just the way I had kept behind Stuart in the last race. Today the roles were reversed, Sharon Stuart and the other runners were keeping pace behind me. I led from the start to the finish, turning up the heat when I chose. As I came to the tape no one could pass me. I'd won gold and it was a fantastic feeling.

An English spectator handed me a Union Jack and I did a lap of honour holding it aloft. The crowd were cheering and applauding. It was the icing on the cake. All the promise that I'd shown in the past years competing in the European Championships and the Olympics had been confirmed. I was the 1990 Commonwealth Games 800 metres gold medallist and no one could ever take that away from me.

Following my silver at the last Commonwealth Games, I'd felt slightly let down that no one seemed to take much notice of what I'd achieved. This time, as the winner, there was a marked difference. Only a couple of days later the English team press officer, Caroline Searle, informed me that David Coleman, the TV sports presenter, would like to see me. I found him in the press area where the commentaries are broadcast. He complimented me on how I'd run my race then asked if I'd like to appear on *A Question of Sport* when we got back to Britain. I'd often watched the programme at home and had no hesitation in saying yes. In a way it was another acknowledgement of what I'd achieved. It was exciting to be asked to take part alongside Ian Botham, Bill Beaumont and some of the other great names of sport.

When it goes out, *A Question of Sport* is edited down to a half hour programme but in the studio it lasts much longer. With all the ribbing and jokes between the teams the game probably lasts over an hour. I enjoyed myself – apart from one embarrassing blunder: I was asked who was the current English record holder for the 800 metres. My mind went blank. I went through a long list trying every name except Shireen Bailey's, which of course was the right answer. It was the last question in the world that I should have got wrong. A few months later I hope I'd have got the answer right since the next English record holder was Diane Edwards!

Returning home from Auckland I was greeted by a small crowd of reporters and cameramen at the airport. There were three of us, Paula Thomas, Ann Williams and myself, returning to Manchester with Commonwealth medals and mine was the only gold. More important to me than the media attention was the sight of my family: Mum, Dad, sisters, brothers, nephews and nieces, all standing at the gate, waving banners and clutching balloons. It was a wonderful welcome to come home to. I felt on top of the world.

I'm glad I couldn't see into the future that day. If anyone had tried to tell me that I'd be coming home from the next Commonwealth Games under a cloud, accused of dope taking, I probably would have laughed in their face.

Chapter 5

Vicente

The first words Vicente ever spoke to me were, 'You have such beautiful, honest eyes, will you marry me?'

'Yes, sure, should we set the date, then?' I laughed.

We were standing outside a hotel in Oslo and had just been introduced. I thought to myself, 'We have a wise guy here who wants to play games', so I played along with him. I didn't know anything about this man. It was only later that I discovered he wasn't playing a joke, he'd spoken in all sincerity.

I was at the Bislett Games once more, this time in July 1990. It had been a good year for me, beginning with my win at the Commonwealth Games, and I was there to run in an important Grand Prix event. The day I was due to race I'd just returned from a loosening jog with Teena Colbrook, an English athlete who lives in America. It was Teena who spotted Vicente standing with a group of Moroccan athletes outside the hotel. She told me he was the manager of Said Aouita, the Moroccan long-distance runner who was widely acknowledged as the best in the world at that time. Teena obviously knew Vicente well because she greeted him with a big hug and a kiss (possibly she had her eye on him!) and then introduced me. I was a bit taken aback by his opening remark. As a chat-up line I thought it was a bit cheap, but then I'd never met anyone who spoke simply and impulsively from the heart like Vicente. He didn't have the barriers and inhibitions that I was used to in British people.

From that first meeting, he hardly let me out of his sight. He arranged to meet me for lunch before my race and, when I was walking through the foyer, he would suddenly appear and suggest that we could eat together that night after the race.

As the Assistant Administrator of the Bislett Games, as well as Aouita's manager, he was very busy that day, but he made time to speak to me.

At first I viewed him as a bit of an inconvenience because I was there to run in a world class race and, as usual, my whole mind was focused on that. The last thing I was looking for was a boyfriend! But Vicente wasn't put off by my initial coolness; he was persistent.

We did meet at lunchtime but it wasn't the cosy twosome he might have wanted since I was sitting with several other British athletes. We exchanged addresses and telephone numbers over the meal and, after Vicente left, a couple of people said, 'You should be careful who you give your address to, I wouldn't give it out like that.'

Vicente had to be with his Moroccan athletes during the day but when I arrived at the track for the evening race, he appeared again. He offered to carry my rucksack and wished me luck in the race. It was an important race for me. The Bislett Games was one of the Grand Prix events and is now known as one of the 'Golden Four' along with Zurich, Brussels and Berlin. Only the top athletes are invited and the field always includes some Olympic or World champions. In the event I came fourth behind Sigrun Wodars, Christine Wachtel and the American Julie Jenkins.

Vicente was one of the first to congratulate me: 'You've run really well.'

'Great, thanks,' I answered.

'No, I think you've run exceptionally well,' he said again. It turned out he was right because I had broken the English 800 metres record, coming home in 1 minute 58.65 seconds.

Vicente had to stay at the meeting to watch his Moroccan athletes running. Later in the evening I saw him back at the hotel. All day he had been saying wonderfully romantic things to me but I wasn't sure how seriously to take him. I'd never heard anyone speak that way before. After the evening meal, which we both ate with other athletes, I announced I was off to bed as I planned to fly home early in the morning. Vicente got up and accompanied me to the lift. As the lift doors opened he leaned down, kissed me softly on the cheek and said good night. The doors closed and I almost sunk to my knees, weak with excitement. At the outset, I'd been quite cautious but from the moment he kissed me I knew I'd never felt like that before. Something special was happening. I ran back to my room and banged on the door. Teena let me in and I blurted out, 'He kissed me! He kissed me!' I sat down on the bed, feeling a quivering wreck. Teena, having lived too long in America, was saying things like, 'He's really got the hots for you, girl! You *must* keep in touch with him.'

The next day I returned home to Manchester whilst Vicente continued on the athletics circuit. From that first meeting he literally phoned me or wrote to me every day.

Soon after I went to St Moritz, spending the first few weeks alone to prepare in altitude for the European Championships later that summer. I hadn't left an address or telephone number but it didn't stop Vicente tracking me down to my hotel (that soon become a trademark of his). I soon found I was beginning to wait expectantly for his phone calls every day. I was there on my own training for two out of three weeks, which can be a lonely experience. The long conversations with Vicente on the telephone were the highlight of my day. We discovered we had so much in common – the same things made us laugh, we had the same single- minded dedication and commitment to athletics, neither of us drank alcohol and we both liked dancing.

I was competing in another of the 'Golden Four' events in Zurich on 15 August and we knew that would be our next chance to meet. When I arrived with the British contingent I found Vicente waiting patiently on a sofa in the hotel foyer. He gave me a present – an ornament with a poem about the greatest feelings of the heart engraved on it. Some men have to try hard to be romantic; I soon realised Vicente wasn't one of them.

When I wasn't preparing for my race or competing we spent every minute of the day together. We hadn't seen each other for a month and had both been anticipating the reunion. We ate our meals together, chatted in the hotel foyer and went for long walks in the evening. It was a new experience to have someone special there encouraging and supporting me before and after the race.

My last race in Europe of the 1990 season was in Rieti, Italy, on 9 September. For some reason Said Aouita pulled out of the competition and normally that would have meant Vicente, as his manager, would not have travelled either. But because it was the last meeting of the year and I was running, he made the journey. Rieti is only a tiny place and quite difficult to reach so he arrived very late the night before my race. We had two days together and it was a time we made 'statements' that we were a couple by holding hands and being affectionate together in public. Throughout the two days, Vicente kept telling me he was coming back to Manchester to be with me. I didn't really believe him until the day I was leaving. Before I boarded my plane he showed me *his* air ticket – it said Rieti to Manchester, one way. We were travelling on different flights but there was no denying now that he was deadly serious about following me. He didn't know a soul in Manchester and certainly had no work to do there. He was travelling half across Europe to a foreign city he hardly knew, just to see more of me. It was flattering and hard to take in.

Vicente asked if I knew of a hotel which had a park nearby where he could go running and keep in training. I said there was a park in Wythenshawe and gave him the telephone number of my best friend, Paula Thomas. I hadn't yet told my parents about Vicente. It wasn't that I thought they wouldn't accept him but it had all happened so fast, in the space of two months. I was probably being a bit over-anxious and protective about the relationship.

Vicente arrived in Manchester and from that day he never actually left, although there was to come a time later when I truly believed I might never see him again. When he arrived at the airport, not knowing anyone in Manchester, he jumped in a taxi and asked the driver to find him a hotel close to a park and not too far from the airport (he knew I lived on that side of the city). He asked for a cheap bed and breakfast but the first two places the driver took him had the doors kicked in and were seedy and run down. Vicente said he'd prefer something of a higher standard (preferably with doors) and ended up at a place called the Horizon Hotel. It wasn't until he telephoned me that we discovered, by sheer chance, he'd ended up about 300 yards from my parents' home.

The Horizon was a basic, no frills hotel with a genial owner who befriended us while Vicente was staying there. He stayed in room number 7 for the next three months, apart from trips away. At the time Vicente had a part-time job as an air steward for Scandinavian Airlines. It was the perfect job for someone in athletics, as he could work during the winter, in close-season, taking time off whenever he wanted. It also meant he could fly all over the world from Manchester and return to see me when he wasn't working. At that point I still had my job at Ron Hill Sports, working three days a week. When I was working and Vicente wasn't, he was left to himself in a city where he was a total stranger and had no friends. He killed time by going for training runs and walking the streets of Manchester to get to know the city I'd grown up in.

When we had time together we would meet at the hotel, either to go training or to go out together like any normal couple. From the day we met, a change started to take place in me. I realised that I'd been so dedicated to my athletics that I was almost addicted to it. I would spend a lot of my free time watching videos of athletics meetings or reading magazines about running and training techniques. It wasn't something that was a chore, I loved athletics and enjoyed anything to do with my sport, but if you asked anyone on the circuit at that time they'd probably have told you that Diane Edwards was dedicated to the point of fanaticism. My friend Paula would say there was nothing I didn't know about athletics.

When Vicente became part of my life I stopped existing and started living. For a long time I'd dreamed of the day I'd walk hand in hand down the street with someone I loved, stopping for a hot chocolate in a café, laughing and chatting, enjoying the small pleasures of life just because we were together. With Vicente, that was just how it was. He was as dedicated as I was to athletics but he also encouraged me to take time out, to go to the cinema or have a meal out together. If we were training, Vicente would time keep for me. Norman Poole was still my coach but if I had to do a session on my own, Vicente would be there to encourage and add a few suggestions to improve my technique. He said a great deal that was new to me – after all, he was working with one of the greatest athletes in the world, Said Aouita, and had trained with the Moroccan record breaker for many years. Vicente's suggestions included things like bounding and weight training in my programme and we discussed race tactics quite a lot. All the same, I didn't always listen to him. I had my own coach in Norman Poole, and we had been very successful together, I wasn't looking for any outside interference. Looking back on it, I realise there was a conflict between my coach and Vicente from the day he came into my life. Their first meeting in London had set the tone – they never really hit it off from the beginning.

Norman, true to past form, was discouraging about the relationship from the outset. He would suggest all kinds of objections – Vicente was from a different culture, I didn't know anything about him, he would upset my routine, we would hardly see each other – all those kinds of things. I was in a very vulnerable position and over the next weeks and months, the pressure started to become unbearable. On the one hand, I had fallen in love and everything I'd ever dreamed of was starting to happen, but on the other, the coach I'd known and respected since I was a teenager was warning me I was putting everything at risk. Some of the things Norman Poole said did make sense to me. It was all happening very quickly, we were already talking about buying a house yet how well *did* we know each other and how could we possibly know what the future held?

Vicente was willing to co-operate with my coach and to do anything that would make the situation easier but I think he realised early on that Norman had such a strong hold on my life that we were heading for a make or break confrontation. Things were to come to a head soon enough and it was almost the end of any future I had dreamt of with Vicente.

Vicente's story

Who was this man who had come into my life during the course of just one day in Oslo? Four years later, when my nightmare began and I was accused of taking steroids, Vicente, by then my coach and husband, was also the victim of rumours and speculation. One tabloid newspaper ran a story calling him the 'Man of Mystery'. The reporter tried to suggest that Vicente was a mysterious figure even to the people who knew him and worked with him. 'Little was known of his past,' the report claimed, implying that Vicente Modahl was the sinister influence behind his wife's downfall.

Vicente was happy to tell his own story to anyone who asked. The idea that my future husband had any mysterious or sinister past is easily cleared up. During the first months we were together in Manchester he told me a lot about his childhood and upbringing in Norway.

Vicente was born in 1960, six years before me, in Bergen, the second largest city in Norway. His father was Spanish and, while studying at a London shipping school to become a sea captain, he met the Norwegian beauty he was to marry. Marit was a model at the time, not only striking to look at but a woman of unusual talents. After the war she was the swimming champion of Scandinavia and by the time Vicente was born she was making a living from teaching.

1968 and still as cute as ever …

All girls together (back left: Doreen; front left: Debra; Di, Barbara and Caroline).

Dipping for the finish line – Anna Wittekind and myself (English Schools 1983). Anna got the verdict.

Photo Eileen Langsley

Running for the finish of the National Cross-Country Championships (1986).

Under 20's Team Tour of Australia and New Zealand (1985). I was Captain.

Posing with Margaret Thatcher after the 1988 Seoul Olympics.

Celebrating with best pal Paula Thomas (nee Dunn) after our success in 1988 Seoul Olympics.
(from left: Paula, Di, my mum and dad – Lena and Sydney).

Meeting Prince Edward with Louise Stewart during the 1990 Commonwealth Games in Auckland.

Paula and I fooling around (as usual) during the closing ceremony of the 1990 Commonwealth Games. Life had a purpose then.

Shortly before receiving my Gold Medal after becoming 1990 Commonwealth Champion. Little did I know that four years later I would not be allowed to defend my title.

Vicente not quite two years old (left) and brother Francisco. Love the tights! Bergen, Norway.

Vicente relaxing in his house in Fuingirola (Spain), 1987.

Father Francisco and son, Valencia 1986.

Vicente and friend Said Aouita – Olympic and World Champion, multi world record holder.

Vicente competing in the Valencia Marathon (Spain), 1986.

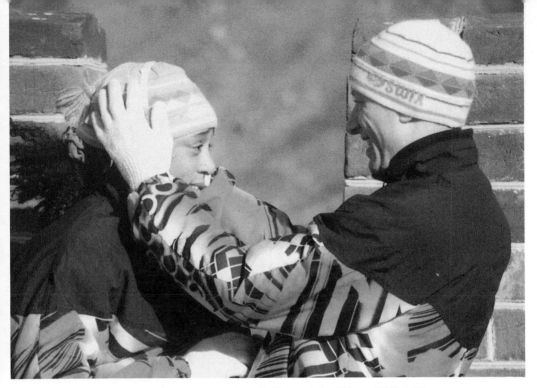

Vicente and I enjoying a trip to Beijing and the Chinese Wall, 1990.

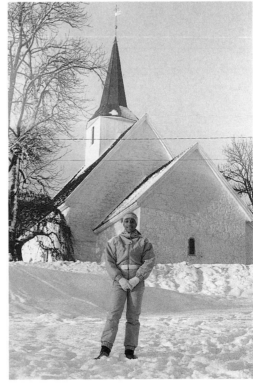

Snow capped and beautiful Norway, 1990.

Anchoring Sale Harriers to win a 4 x 400m
in the UK League.

Recovering from injury in 1991 . . . running in water

Preparing for the Barcelona Olympics at high altitude in
the Atlas Mountains of Morocco, 1992.

'Feet behind the line!' Starting off a road race for a
local school, 1991.

Vicente's childhood couldn't have been more different from my own upbringing on a Manchester council estate. From the age of 1 he lived on a remote island, only connected to the mainland by steamship. Even in the 1960s the island had only one road, mostly used by horses and carriages. The islanders were farmers and fishermen and the school where Vicente's mother taught was the centre of the community. While I was out playing chase at the end of the city cul-de-sac where we lived, Vicente and his brothers grew up arm in arm with Nature. Sometimes they would sleep out in the forest or build a snow cave where they could stay warm inside. There were nine children in the family – seven brothers and two sisters – and all of them learnt to swim, fish and ski from an early age. At the age of 7 Vicente would take a boat out early in the morning to set his fishing nets before school. His parents divorced when he was 7, leaving Vicente's mother the task of bringing up nine children on her own. She was a proud, hard-working woman who wouldn't accept help from anyone else, financial or otherwise. She taught her children the value of honesty and hard work if they wanted to achieve anything in life.

Right from an early age it was clear what Vicente wanted to achieve. Sport meant everything to him. Like me, he started by running in races with family and friends which his brother organised around the house. Then, when he was only 6 years old, he was allowed to compete in a 60 metres race with children a year older. He had listened to athletics on the radio, to the roar of the crowd and the commentator's voice rising in pitch as the race reached its climax, and now he was lining up in his first race with a number pinned on his chest. The gun going off frightened him and he crossed the line last – he didn't know how to sprint like the older boys – but he'd taken part and was given a small silver cup. He carried it home proudly and knew he was hooked on athletics for life.

At the tender age of 6 he had begun training with his older brother and a year later had won his first competition: a road race of 1000 metres. Again he was running against boys two years his senior but his strongest memory of the race was seeing a boy cheat. They were approaching the half way point when a boy in front cut a corner, gaining about twenty metres. That made Vicente so angry inside that he was determined not to lose to anyone who cheated. He wanted to be able to win the race the way the athletes did it on the radio and television, win because you were fast and you'd given everything. He knew if you cheated, you cheated yourself because that pride in what you'd achieved would be lost for ever.

In 1973, when Vicente was 13, he visited the Bislett Games (where we would meet years later) for the first time. Somehow he managed to sneak on to the arena and get the autograph of John Akii-bua, the Ugandan 400 metres hurdles Olympic champion. Akii-bua and Benjamin Jipsho befriended their young fan and let him sit beside them during the Games. They even escorted him round the track, introducing him to other famous athletes so that he could add their autographs to his book. That day Vicente met Olympic and World champions in person, and knew that one day he wanted to follow in their footsteps. As a long-distance runner, the steeplechase was the event he chose to make his mark.

During his teenage years he started to grow alarmingly, but a beanpole physique was not suited to distance running. If it wasn't for the encouragement of Martin Hole, an international cross-country ski champion, he might have given up. Hole told him, 'You can't stop running, you have such a beautiful stride. Ski with me once a day and then you can run once a day. You'll soon see the changes.' Martin Hole was right; by the age of 20, Vicente was the best young 2000 metres steeplechaser in Scandinavia, taking three gold medals at the National Norwegian Junior Championships. He progressed to the senior ranks and claimed a place among the top five Norwegians in the 3000 metres steeplechase during the early 1980s – when I was just starting my career with Sale Harriers.

During the 1980s two things happened to divert Vicente away from his ambition to be an Olympic champion. One was a disastrous incident with a gang of youths in Oslo, the other was meeting Said Aouita.

In 1982 Vicente went to Mexico City for altitude training. It was an impulse to go there but one that changed the direction of his whole life. He met two Moroccan athletes there and was asked to translate for them, as the only person at the camp who could speak French. One of the Moroccans introduced himself as Said Aouita (a name that meant nothing at the time) and the other was called Fousi Lahbi. Vicente soon struck up a friendship with them. They had rooms next door and became so close that they would borrow each other's clothes. It soon became clear that Said Aouita had extraordinary confidence and ambition. Even as an unknown he would maintain, 'I'm going to break world records, beat Coe, Ovett and Cram and be the number one in the world.' Most of the athletes and coaches at the camp thought he was crazy, he was training like a maniac and was never going to achieve anything. Vicente was the only one who accepted him as he was and watched what he was doing.

Said had developed a training system which was new and all his own. Instead of running a session of twenty laps with a recovery in between, the typical approach in distance training, he sometimes ran ten, six or even four laps – but the difference was in the speed: he was running them fast and changing pace all the time. One day in Mexico Vicente timed him on the training track. Aouita ran ten laps with 90 seconds recovery between each one. His average time was 54.5 seconds in altitude. When Vicente showed him the times he was delighted. He had read in a magazine that the best session Sebastian Coe had done was ten laps in 55.5 seconds – he had just beaten that. To the Moroccan it was further proof that he was going to be the best in the world. From that day Vicente started to believe in him; Said Aouita was one day going to be a revelation in the world of athletics. Said wanted his new friend to help all the time with sprint training, endurance or middle-distance running, but whatever they did together, Said was better. At the age of 23, Vicente had encountered one of the world's great runners and he realised that his own talent wasn't in the same class. He could be a good runner but he would never be a Said Aouita.

Vicente believes his own career started to nose dive from that time. Even in Mexico he started to neglect his own training for the chance to get more involved on the coaching side as a friend and training partner. It was a loose arrangement but the start of the road that later led him to become the coach and agent of many international athletes – including myself.

Said Aouita didn't take long to make his entrance on the world stage. Later that year he took the bronze medal in the World Championships in 1983, losing to Steve Cram and Steve Scott after a tactical mistake. Suddenly Vicente was talking to him on the phone almost every week. From 1985 they started to travel together to championships and training camps. It was still on an unofficial, friendly basis but a year later Said started to ask Vicente to become his manager. Vicente didn't think he could do the job at first but in time he was to change his mind.

One decisive factor was an incident that effectively put an end to his running career. During the mid 1980s, he had struggled with injuries and felt he was going nowhere. Then in 1987 he experienced a late spring and came back into form, finishing second in an international between Norway and England. He'd set a new personal best time and started to dream again of the Olympics.

A week later Vicente was in a small park in Oslo behind the National Theatre. He'd just heard the news that he'd been selected for the Norwegian national team. It was a warm evening and he was sharing a bench with another athlete. They were killing time before going to see a film. There was no reason to expect anything unusual on such a peaceful evening. Then a street gang appeared coming that way. They wore jeans and jackets and one had a red bandana tied round his head. All were unshaven, dirty and had an unfocused look about the eyes that suggested they were on drugs. Vicente had seen plenty of drug addicts before; during his military service he was one of the King's Guard and heroin addicts were often found loitering in the gardens surrounding the royal castle in Oslo. He avoided looking at the street gang. They were approaching strangers in the street aggressively and one of them stopped by the bench where Vicente sat. The youth leaned towards him.

'Got a light?'

'Sorry, I haven't. I don't smoke.'

Before he knew what was happening, three of the gang were behind the bench and pulling Vicente up by the arms. They dragged him away from his friends and started to attack him, punching his face and body and kicking his legs. Vicente fought back as best he could, knocking some of them to the ground. But his left knee had received a painful kick and he found he could hardly stand on it. Out of the corner of his eye he saw a taxi parked about twenty metres away. He limped towards it, shouting to the driver to drive off as he flung himself in. Lying in the back, he felt bruised all over his body, his face was bleeding and his ribs and knee were too sore to move.

The police later took him back to identify the gang who'd assaulted him. They found the culprits still on the street, but the policeman merely shrugged. 'Drug addicts. We've been watching them every night. No use arresting them, they'd only be out in the morning.'

Vicente was incredulous. 'You mean they attacked me for no reason and you can't arrest them?'

'Sorry. You're not badly injured enough. If they do something serious we'll put them away for a long time but we have to wait till that happens.'

'You're saying that if I'd been stabbed with a knife, if I was dying, that would be good enough?'

'Don't blame us. It's the court system. Come on, we'll drop you at the hospital.' Vicente had broken ribs, broken toes and a kneecap so badly smashed that he didn't run again for eighteen months. Even today his knee can only cope with light training. It dashed his hopes of running for Norway and, as it turned out, brought a premature end to his athletics career.

Instead Vicente turned back to his friendship with Said Aouita and his growing interest in coaching. During 1988–9 he attended a lot of competitions with Aouita, still helping out on a friendly basis. In the six years he'd known the Moroccan champion he'd learned how a world-class athlete trains and prepares, how he negotiates with organisers and sponsors and how he stays at the top. Without planning it, Vicente had acquired all the information he needed to become a top coach and manager in athletics. When, in 1989, Said asked him a third time to be his manager, Vicente said yes.

Their professional relationship was based on trust and a mutual friendship. Once, when Vicente was feeling low and depressed following his knee injury, Said telephoned him late one night and insisted on travelling to see him the next day to make sure his friend was all right. Vicente would say that Said was closer to him than his own family. Said had made an enormous impact on his life and direction; Vicente, in turn, dedicated all his time and energy to further Said Aouita's career. He was glad to do it because he loved to see Said racing. How many people get the chance to be the best friend and manager to one of the greatest athletes in the world, possibly in the history of distance running?

Vicente had been Said's manager for around a year when he met me at the 1990 Bislett Games. Said Aouita didn't run that year but Vicente was there with his other Moroccan athletes and as the assistant organiser of the Bislett Games. It was one of the happiest periods in his life. He was helping to run one of the most prestigious meets in the world, he was the manager of Said Aouita and then he met me and fell in love. Everything should have been perfect and complete for us during that time. Instead, we found our relationship coming under terrible strain from both sides. I had Norman Poole warning me to be careful and not to risk everything I'd built in my career, and Vicente had Said Aouita.

Said was taking the whole thing badly. He said that Vicente couldn't work with him and be with me at the same time. He'd been used to having his friend's total devotion both as manager and travelling companion; now someone else was threatening to take first place. The friction caused by Vicente's relationship with me was building towards inevitable confrontation.

I had one more domestic meeting at the end of the 1990 season. It was held in Sheffield. I was going with my coach and I knew Vicente would be there with Said Aouita. I was dreading the day. I felt I was in the middle of a situation that was becoming too stressful to cope with. Vicente and I had just enjoyed a wonderful week together in Manchester but I knew I'd have to virtually ignore him at Sheffield in order to avoid tensions with Norman Poole or Said. I had another reason for dreading the day too: in my pocket was a letter I'd written telling Vicente that our relationship was over.

Anyone outside the situation may find it hard to understand my decision but the pressure on me at that time was unbearable. I really didn't know what to do and had spent many hours talking over the situation with Paula. It seemed to come down to a choice between the familiar and the unknown. Should I break up the security and routine of my present life, my dedication as an athlete and my successful partnership with my coach, for something that was an unknown future? I knew I loved Vicente but I didn't know what sort of life lay ahead for us. I knew what I was familiar with. And all the time Norman Poole was warning me that I could be making a big mistake. I was his best athlete at the time, he had coached me to the point where I was the Commonwealth champion and English 800 metres record holder. Vicente on the other hand was manager and friend to one of the best athletes in the world. Norman Poole may have thought it inevitable that I'd start to listen to my husband more and more if we got married and his position as my coach would be threatened.

Vicente's argument was simple and could be put into three words – he loved me. He didn't have any money, a house or a big yacht, but he loved me and my athletics career was just as important to him as it was to me.

The day of the Sheffield meet dawned and I went with the letter to Vicente burning a hole in my pocket. Before the race Norman and I were in the warm-up area with Vicente and Said Aouita close by. Everything was going on as normal around us but the atmosphere was heavy with tension. Vicente and I were unable even to talk to one another, I could only sneak a glance in his direction every now and then. How I managed to race that evening I will never know. It wasn't until all the events had finished that I could finally sit down to chat briefly with Vicente. Even then I was conscious of Norman Poole in the background looking angry and impatient.

I took out the letter and gave it to Vicente, asking him not to read it until I'd gone. He looked distressed. 'Why not? Why not?' he asked. 'I want to open it.' Vicente is the kind of person who cannot wait to hear something later, you must tell him then or not at all. Nevertheless, I left him the letter and somehow managed to tear myself away. Inside the envelope were two or three pages saying how wonderful our relationship had been, how my life was richer and fuller since I'd known him. Everything I wrote in the letter was positive until the last sentence which said we had to finish, it wouldn't work.

I went home from the meeting feeling desolate. I genuinely feared that I might never see Vicente again after that evening. He told me that Scandinavian Airlines had offered him a job in Singapore for six months; if our relationship didn't work out he was going to accept the offer. The more I thought about it on the journey home the more I began to question the sense of what I was doing. It felt that if I sent Vicente away I'd be sentencing myself to a grey existence for the rest of my life. Nobody could ever make me feel again the way I'd felt in the last few months.

When I reached home I called Paula from my parents' house and told her I'd finished with Vicente.

'Oh Di, did you?'

'Yes but I think that I might have made a big mistake.'

'What do you mean?'

'I don't think I really want to end it.'

I went on to pour out my predicament. I had no idea how I could get in touch with Vicente because he was going to Singapore. I'd burnt my boats and didn't know how to bring them back. I told Paula that if by any chance Vicente called her (they were good friends by then) that she must tell him to contact me immediately and come back.

Vicente was in fact intending to take the airline job in Singapore, having read my letter. But first he accompanied Said Aouita to New York in late September 1990 where the Moroccan was to compete in the Fifth Avenue Mile. They stayed in the Holiday Inn on Times Square. Vicente was utterly miserable, while Said was delighted to have his friend and manager back.

What saved the situation was a phone call. A few days later Vicente, on an impulse, phoned my best friend, Paula. He says the conversation went something like this: 'I just called to ask you to tell Diane that I'm sorry I messed up her life so much. If it was up to me I would have stood by what I said and married her. I know that losing her is the worst thing that has ever happened . . .'

'Oh, stop talking!' Paula interrupted. 'Just phone Diane.'

'Why? What do you mean?'

'She's been on the phone to me every day crying her eyes out. She wants to see you.'

'But she told me she never wanted to see me again.'

'So? She lied!'

I was at work when Vicente called me. I think I screamed down the phone, I was so happy and relieved to hear his voice again. I told him he must never go away again (though I admit I'd been the one who'd told him to go!) He sounded unsure at first, he wanted to be certain I knew what I wanted this time. We couldn't go back to the old situation, he said. Whatever problems we were facing we'd have to face them together. I replied that I knew what I wanted – to marry him. When was he coming back to England? I came off the phone feeling as if I was walking on air. We were together again and everything would be all right.

Meanwhile in New York, Vicente's happy news sparked off a terrible row with Said Aouita. One that put an end to their friendship for good. Since they'd arrived in New York, Said had done his best to comfort Vicente, although he couldn't conceal the fact that he was happy that the split had taken place. Only the night before they'd been at dinner with Steve Cram, Peter Elliot, and the American, Steve Scott. Said had been telling them all how important Vicente was for his career.

When Vicente came off the phone and told Said that he was back together with me, Said exploded with rage. He said it was time to choose between him and me. If Vicente chose to stay with him then the world was his oyster, he could have anything he wanted. If he chose me then Said would never work with him again. Vicente tried to be reasonable at first. He said that it didn't have to be a choice. He wanted to marry me and to carry on working with Said. But that only made the Moroccan athlete more angry. He kept repeating the choice – to stay with him or to marry me. When Vicente continued to maintain that he would do both, Said lost his temper completely. He threw a glass which missed Vicente narrowly and shattered against the wall. Vicente had been initially shocked by his friend's reaction but now he was furious himself.

'Who do you think you are?' Vicente shouted. 'We've been best friends for nine years and now you're telling me I can't have a life! What kind of friendship is that? I am going to marry Diane and that's the end of it.'

The row ended with Said threatening to ruin Vicente's reputation in athletics. He would tell people that Vicente had never been his manager, training partner or friend, he was no more than a bell boy – someone to carry his bag.

Vicente replied, 'If that is the level you have sunk to then I can't be your friend any more.'

That was the last time they ever spoke to each other. Vicente had to make two great sacrifices to be with me, he gave up his friendship with Said Aouita and his job as manager to the best distance athlete in the world. Today, despite the sad way things ended, Vicente still thinks of Said as the best friend he ever had. He sees the Moroccan athlete as a Jekyll and Hyde character capable of extraordinary good and equal bad. Whatever their differences he was Vicente's best friend who would go to any lengths to help him up if he was down. He was also arguably one of the greatest distance runners of all time. He covered events from the 800 to 10,000 metres and won medals or broke records in almost everything he went in for.

I knew nothing about the break with Said until some time later. All I could think about was when I'd see Vicente again. He was on the other side of the Atlantic and supposed to be going on from New York to Los Angeles, so I was impatient. As it turned out I didn't have to wait very long. Paula called me at work and suggested we go out for a Chinese meal with another friend. We had a lot to talk about, so I readily agreed. I spoke to Vicente later that afternoon in New York and told him I was going out that evening, so not to call.

When I arrived at the restaurant in Chinatown I was late. There was no sign of Paula, which was puzzling and annoying. I was shown to a table and sat down. A waiter came to my table and hovered behind me. He asked if I knew what I wanted to eat. I replied, 'No thanks, I'm waiting for somebody.'

'Can I get you something to drink?'

'No I don't want anything yet, thank you.'

He was a persistent waiter. Next he leaned over and pointed to something on the menu, recommending me to try it. Something in the voice made me look up. I jumped out of my seat, took a few steps back and screamed, 'What are you doing here?'

Vicente was standing at my table, dressed as a waiter. I was totally stunned. I'd only spoken to him in New York nine hours earlier, how could he be standing here in Manchester?

We sat together and ate the food, not really tasting it, while he told me how he'd planned his surprise. The meeting at the restaurant had all been arranged with Paula simply as a ploy to get me there. He had arranged it all two hours before flying to Manchester and had spoken to me by phone from the airport. He landed at Manchester Airport 45 minutes before the table was booked and made a mad taxi dash to the restaurant. Fortunately I was late, so he had time to hide his bags and persuade the waiter to let him borrow a jacket and a menu to give his girlfriend a surprise. It had all worked perfectly, giving me the shock of my life. It was typical of Vicente. He was always full of surprises. He'd rushed back half way across the world because he couldn't wait another day to see me.

That evening was like a new start for us. I had committed myself to Vicente and I knew he had never stopped loving me through all the upheaval we'd been through. He told me about the row with Said Aouita and that he now only had his job at the airline. It didn't matter. We were a young couple in love and looking forward to the future, full of hope and anticipation. It seemed to us we'd already weathered our fair share of stress and heartache – but we could have no idea of what lay in store up ahead.

Chapter 6

Breakaway

Once I'd made up my mind that I wanted to be with Vicente, life became simpler. I spent all my time with the man I intended to marry. In the winter of 1990 we moved in to live with my family while we looked for our own place to buy. I had saved quite a bit from working at the sports company and Vicente was flying with Scandinavian Airlines while he tried to build up a group of athletes in Britain to manage.

Norman Poole was still my coach and told me he was very happy that the relationship with Vicente was working out. He always gave me the impression that he was getting on with Vicente but when we returned from training at Sale Harriers, I would hear a different story of what had been said. It took a long time before I realised how much was going on behind my back. Looking back on it, from the moment I met Vicente, the situation with Norman Poole became more and more impossible.

There was no such problem between Vicente and my parents, who got on well from the first day they met. We ended up living with them for three months. They could see that I was ecstatically happy. I was still dedicated to athletics but my life was blossoming in new ways.

In December 1990 I had my first experience of a Norwegian Christmas. It was something that became a tradition for us over the years, but I will never forget the first time I went. Just before we left England I remember looking out of the window at my parents' house in Sale and calling to Vicente, 'Oh come and look, it's snowing!' Vicente came to the window and just laughed out loud. 'Snow? That's not snow!' I was insulted. 'Of course it's snow, it's fantastic, we can build a snowman.'

'When we get to Norway you'll see real snow,' he promised.

Later we heard reports on the television of lorries in Britain jack-knifed on the motorways and drivers trapped in their cars. Vicente was dumbfounded – all this because of a light sprinkling of snow!

I had agreed to go to Norway that winter on the usual condition that I was still able to train. (I hadn't become so relaxed about running that I could take time off before Christmas!) Vicente had assured me that training wouldn't be a problem. He was so anxious that everything on my first visit should be just right that he went on ahead to make preparations.

When I arrived in Norway we arranged that he would pick me up at the airport. On his way to meet me he drove his brother's car through the steadily falling snow. His mind was back in Manchester reliving all the incredible events of the last few months. Suddenly he was jolted back into the present. A car appeared round the bend in front driving on the same side of the road. Vicente slammed on the brakes – but too late – they smashed head on. Fortunately both drivers were unscathed by the collision and they climbed out of their cars.

'What do you think you were doing?' Vicente demanded angrily. 'You were driving on the wrong side of the road!'

The other driver stared at him in disbelief. '*You* were driving on the wrong side of the road!' Vicente looked back at the crumpled wreckage of his brother's car and realised the truth. He'd been living in Manchester so long and his mind had been so full of meeting his English girlfriend, that he'd been driving on the left-hand side of the road. He ended up having to hire a car to meet me at the airport. That wasn't the end of our problems. We went straight from the airport to the training track. When we arrived I began to see what Vicente meant about real snow in Norway. It was about six inches deep! Vicente was looking embarrassed and uncomfortable. 'There wasn't that much snow earlier this afternoon,' he muttered weakly. In fact it must have been snowing steadily for hours because the track was covered. I guessed he didn't want to tell me as I might have cancelled the trip if I couldn't train.

We did go ahead with the training session; Vicente was determined to keep his promise. At one point I slipped and fell and he was by my side immediately, nervous that I might have injured myself. It was not the perfect introduction to Norway he'd planned, but we could see the funny side later. In any case, he needn't have worried, I soon fell in love with his country. It was far more beautiful than I'd ever imagined. We stayed that night with Vicente's brother. During the night I remember getting up when the whole house was silent and everyone asleep. I pulled back the curtains to look out of the window. It was just before Christmas and the snow glistened on the fir trees and covered the ground in a deep white carpet. All the nearby houses were illuminated by lights outside and each had a Christmas star shining in the window. I stood looking out the window at this enchanted scene for a long long time, and I was sure I could make out a big snowman standing alone in the middle of the forest.

After that year a Norwegian Christmas became a regular event for us. It was different altogether from the English traditions I was used to. In Norway Christmas Day is celebrated on 24 December. Breakfast and lunch are light to prepare you for *Pinnekjott* (pronounced Pinnishut), the wonderful meal which is waiting in the evening. The main dish is smoked lamb ribs which has been prepared months beforehand. The smoked and salted meat is cooked in the pan for hours with birchwood to give it a distinctive aromatic flavour. Normally all nine of Vicente's brothers and sisters would be sitting around the table with their partners and children. Later we open the presents and sit around talking into the night. The next day, our Christmas Day, everyone goes cross-country skiing to make up for the excess they've eaten. On my first attempt I ended up on my back in the snow quite a few times. Vicente had to hold on to me when we went downhill, I'm not one for a roller coaster ride – going over a hill in the car is usually enough to turn my stomach!

On our visits over the next few years we did many of the things Vicente had described to me in his childhood. Once we went fishing in a rowing boat and sat in the middle of a fjord with the water smooth as a mirror reflecting the green mountains all round us. Another time we went running at night along one of Vicente's old routes. The darkness all round was absolutely pitch black, which was quite frightening for someone like me used to running on pavements and parks in a big city.

It was on a winter run back in England that I picked up an injury that was to ruin the whole of the 1991 season. I was running a cross-country race on a very hilly course which had frozen over the night before. I hadn't anticipated the harsh conditions and wore 9 mm spikes for the race. It felt like running on concrete and at one point I felt a pain around the area of my shin. In training afterwards the pain would come and go. Despite treatment with ultra-sound and massage it began to get more inflamed. Eventually I went for a bone scan at Hope Hospital which showed that I had two stress fractures in my left tibia.

The news was devastating as the World Championships were due to be held in Tokyo that summer. The problem wasn't diagnosed until early in the New Year and I was told the only remedy was rest. Neither Vicente nor I was willing to accept that I was out of the World Championships and we determined to try everything possible to get me fit. Vicente suggested a Norwegian training method which involved running in water using an aqua-vest. The idea is to simulate training in a tank or swimming pool, wearing the vest to keep you afloat. It has the same cardiovascular effect as running, whilst protecting the injury because the water bears your weight. By that point we had bought a house in Sale and I went to the local Leisure Centre every morning at 7 am to run in the pool. Vicente was always the one there, pushing and encouraging me at these sessions.

Training progressed slowly and I could still feel the crack in my bone for a long time. By the time of the World Championship trials I was still pigheadedly clinging to the hope that I could qualify. In races I had been beaten by almost every English girl that year. The trials were in Birmingham and were a disaster – I came in sixth. Having been the winner at the National Championships for the last four years, it was a humiliating experience. Vicente and I had believed that we'd put so much time into training in the pool that I would be successful. But only so much can be simulated in water. If you want to run to the highest standard, you also need to train and race on a track. The trials had come too soon for me and I'd simply run out of time. Those were the first championships since 1986 I'd been forced to sit at home and watch on television.

Ironically, I finished the 1991 season well. In September I ran a race in Koblenz against a field including many athletes who'd taken part in the World Championships. The race was also important because I tried out a new tactic that Vicente had worked on with me. The plan was to change pace in the last 120 metres. Previously I would have battled all the way in to the line, but this time there was a concerted effort to up the pace at a certain point in the race. At the 120 metres point I was lying around fourth. I dug down to my reserves and went into another gear, coming from behind to win the race.

The prize was a bottle of champagne which we decided to save for our wedding. It was like a consolation reward for both of us. We had endured a frustrating year in which I'd put myself on the line and lost publicly over and over again.

Vicente had supervised my training throughout the injury and it was his idea to introduce the change of pace that won me the race in Koblenz. But at that stage I wasn't looking at him as my coach, nor was it ever his intention to take on that role. As my fiancé he was frustrated at some of the things he saw missing in my training schedule. His experience of working with one of the world's best athletes meant he found it impossible to sit back and watch mistakes being made without saying anything. He wanted to work with Norman Poole and discuss how my strength and technique could be improved, but Norman made it clear he didn't welcome any outside influence – or interference, as he probably regarded it.

I was happy to continue with my present coach. My track record before I met Vicente spoke for itself – Olympic finalist, Commonwealth champion, English 800 metres record holder – it had all been achieved with Norman Poole coaching me, so why change a winning formula? I had a coach who'd known me for years and knew how to prepare me, I certainly wasn't convinced that Vicente knew everything. One objection was that he had never coached a female athlete before. I was learning fast that his style of training was very different to Norman Poole's; it was much more geared towards championship racing. Vicente prepared his athletes by training specifically for three hard races in three days, which is what you face at a major championship. He would point this out but I would argue that I didn't want to be worn out.

If I mentioned to Norman that there might be certain elements missing from my training he would react strongly and have an answer to every issue. The triangle was still operating with me caught in the middle. The undercurrents were building up towards the following year, which coincided with the Olympics.

Throughout the 1992 season tension and conflict were never far from the surface. I started to consider the question seriously: should I make a choice between Norman Poole and Vicente as my coach?

I had lost a season through injury but there was no reason to think that I couldn't get back to my best form. In Seoul four years previously I had qualified as a finalist against everyone's expectations and this time I was going to the Olympics as a much more experienced athlete. In order to make up all the ground I had lost through my injury in 1991, I trained right through the close season. I arrived in Barcelona for the Olympics in good spirits and feeling confident. My racing had gone well that season and as the undisputed British number one, I didn't have to compete in the 800 metres national trials, opting to run the 400 metres instead. The Olympic qualifying heat went according to plan and I finished comfortably third, crossing the tape with the defending Olympic champion, Sigrun Wodars of East Germany.

The day of the Olympic semi-final arrived. I was keyed up but confident I could make the final by taking one of the top four places. The race started well and I was in an ideal position as we went through the bell for the final lap. As we took the bend, there were a lot of athletes bunched together and somebody pushed me in the back. I lost my stride pattern and, from that point, I never really recovered. The other runners had gone ahead and I wasn't able to get back into the race. Having reached the final in my first Olympics it was a bitter disappointment not to get beyond the semi-final in Barcelona.

With hindsight, there may have been other factors at work. I wasn't strong enough mentally or physically during that summer to cope with the kind of rough ride you sometimes get in an Olympic semi-final. All the stress and tension of the situation with Norman Poole and Vicente was taking its toll on me. During the whole year, although I'd run well at times, I knew something wasn't quite right. At the end of the season I finally made the decision I'd put off for so long. I told Norman Poole that I didn't want him to coach me any more. My reasons weren't new, I had simply reached the conclusion that Vicente was right – something was missing from my training. We had talked about these missing elements for a long time, things like changing pace, race tactics and strength training such as bounding. It was true that Norman

Poole did give me race tactics but they were general rather than specific. His argument against bounding was that I risked injury, all my family had weak lower legs, he said, and the stress fracture I'd suffered only proved this. I did do circuit training but it wasn't specifically geared to power and explosive strength which were the very things needed for 800 metres running. Norman had an explanation for everything Vicente or I suggested, so nothing changed.

Not surprisingly, my decision to split with Norman wasn't popular. I continued to train at Sale Harriers where Norman is a coach, but for a long time I felt that there was an odd atmosphere whenever Vicente and I arrived.

But 1992 didn't end on a sour note as there was one joyful occasion left. On 19 September, six weeks after the Olympics, Vicente and I got married. It was a day that my husband says I planned with military precision. I'd left my job at Ron Hill Sports earlier that year and I had time on my hands to make all the arrangements before Barcelona. With Vicente's Norwegian family and his Spanish father coming, together with my parents' Jamaican relatives, we had all the makings of a wonderful international celebration.

I had planned the day in so much detail that I wanted everything to be perfect. Naturally something went wrong right at the start. I forgot my bouquet and didn't realise until we'd nearly reached the church. The car had to turn round and drive home, making us late for the service. When we finally arrived, my brothers and the two bridesmaids were waiting outside, wondering what had delayed us. Howard and Clive went straight in the church and sat down. Unfortunately they shut the two heavy church doors behind them, leaving me outside, hands full of flowers and two bridesmaids asking why we didn't go in. Everybody inside the church must have wondered who it was banging on the doors.

We finally got inside and began to process down the aisle. As we walked, I gave my Dad a dig in the ribs and he knew immediately that it meant, 'Slow down!' For weeks I'd been reminding him that he had to walk slowly so that I could savour the moment. Vicente was waiting for me at the front, looking so pale and nervous that I hardly recognised him. He probably thought by this time that I wasn't coming. But I was the one getting stressed and he did his best to calm me down throughout the day. The problem was my dress. It was a traditional dress with a seven foot veil and needed the air to flow underneath so that it would puff out properly. Following the marriage service we all went into the church garden for the photographs.

'Does my dress look all right?' I asked Vicente.

'It looks fine.'

'Can you just fluff it for me please?'

He bent down and prodded it around a bit. I looked daggers at him.

'That's not done properly,' I hissed. 'Get Doreen, she knows how to do it.'

My oldest sister and chief bridesmaid, Doreen, was summoned and commanded to fluff my dress. All day Doreen had the task of running around after me making sure that the dress was 'fluffed' to my satisfaction.

The reception was a colourful, noisy affair. Vicente's family have no problem letting their hair down on a big occasion. There was a lot of cheering, singing and calling out. At one point Vicente and I were requested to carry out the Norwegian tradition of standing on our chairs to give each other a big hug and a kiss. Vicente nudged me and whispered, 'I haven't heard of this one before.' It was another joke his family had just made up on the day. The Norwegian contingent then tried to teach the English some of their traditional wedding songs which caused much helpless laughter on both sides. In the evening there was dancing. Vicente and I did a Spanish Lambada dance in honour of his father. A steel band began to play calypso to introduce a Caribbean element, and we invited the guests to try limbo dancing. The celebrations went on late into the evening and, when we retired to the bridal suite, it was to find cornflakes in our bed and plastic ducks, bearing good luck messages, floating in the jacuzzis.

Our honeymoon was four days in Los Angeles and the rest on Maui, one of the less populated Hawaiian islands. I was determined that I was going to take the infamous wedding dress on our honeymoon, despite all Vicente's protests about luggage space. From my childhood I had always had an ambition to run along a beach in my wedding dress – this was my chance to fulfil my dream.

When we were on the beach one day I put my wedding dress

on over my swimming costume (unfortunately Doreen couldn't be there to fluff it) and Vicente's job was to take photographs and hold the video camera. I must have looked insane running around on the sand in a long white wedding gown, waving some roses that Vicente had picked. People were staring open-mouthed as I splashed through the shallows. They probably thought it was a photo shoot for a bridal magazine.

We got the photos developed the next day and – disaster – they hadn't come out. Vicente said, 'Never mind, at least we tried.'

I stared at him. 'What do you mean, we tried? We'll just have to get some more film and do it again.'

The next day we went through the whole pantomime a second time: the wedding dress in the boot of the car, Vicente pinching roses off a nearby bush and me running around in my beautiful wedding dress getting it covered in sand and salt water. The photos were developed again and again they didn't come out. The same thing happened the third and the fourth day – I don't give up easily! There was a couple who went for a walk every morning at that time and they must have thought Vicente was wonderfully romantic, picking fresh roses for his wife every day. By the fourth time we realised that there had been a fault with the camera all along. We did get some pictures in the end and the video made hilarious viewing once we got home. There are all the holiday makers relaxing on the golden sand in Hawaii, when suddenly a mad figure comes into view, running at the sea's edge, trailing a long soggy white dress and brandishing a bunch of roses!

Even on honeymoon we didn't stop training completely. It wasn't a strict regime but we wanted to keep in shape because Barcelona had been such a disappointment. We were determined that next year would be a better season. I'd gained a new husband and a new coach in the space of a few months, my life was entering a new phase.

Chapter 7

My Husband, My Coach

The year 1993 dawned with Vicente completely in charge as my coach. It wasn't hard to see the difference in my new training regime, only time would reveal whether my performances on the track also showed a difference. Vicente's approach to training was much stricter in the sense that he expected definite results. In the past I had a good day's training if I felt good and I ran indifferently if I wasn't feeling good. With my new regime, I went to the training track knowing exactly what was expected of me in the times I should run. The idea was to run with a time clearly before me as a target. If I didn't make the time, that didn't in a sense matter, the whole point was to put in the effort, to achieve my full potential. There was no room any more for training hard and 'hoping for the best'. The times Vicente set were geared to championship racing, so if I was aiming to run two minutes in an 800 metres race I would be training at a faster pace than that beforehand.

One other crucial change Vicente introduced was the idea of keeping back a reserve. Even though I was running hard, I never allowed myself to reach rock bottom, there always had to be that extra edge there as I came off the final bend. Previously I would have gone flat out all the way to the line, or at the other extreme, run too comfortably; this way I knew mentally and physically that I'd kept something back for the last crucial stage.

The difference in my new training was one of precision. Before I had trained as a good all round athlete, capable of producing results on my day at British or possibly European standard, but not consistently at world-class level. With Vicente coaching, all my training was geared to championship racing. In a championship you run a heat, the semi-final the next day and then the final after a day's break. Three gruelling races in four days. In training I would mirror that sequence. Every ten days we'd perform a key session which was in effect three races over four days. At the end of it I knew exactly how far behind or how far ahead I was in my preparation. Previously I had never been fit enough to cope with three races in four days and usually I had blown out on the third race.

People have asked me what it's like to be coached by my husband. The short answer is that when we are on the track Vicente is in charge, whereas in our marriage there is obviously a lot more discussion and compromise! On the track, if Vicente said, 'You're doing another lap' or 'We're doing a weight session today', then I did it. Anyone who wants to get to the top in athletics has to respect the coach's opinion and his/her decisions. All too often athletes become introspective and unable to see their progress objectively. We forget very quickly that we were running well a week ago; the fact that we feel shattered today means the whole season is a disaster! A coach takes the longer-term view and can see when the athlete is still on target.

Having said this, I didn't slip into my new coaching regime like putting on a comfortable pair of slippers. There were arguments and conflicts to begin with – anyone who thinks I'm a meek little woman with no opinions of my own, doesn't know me well. Whereas Norman Poole had coached me from a naive teenager, Vicente was taking on a Commonwealth gold medallist and Olympic finalist. I thought I had some experience of how Diane Edwards (now Modahl) ran best and I didn't accept all Vicente's changes overnight. Initially I would argue quite angrily. I would say, 'I won't be able to train three hard days consecutively, I'll be shattered' or 'Why should I keep a reserve? Why don't I just run as I feel and, if I'm feeling good, just push it really hard?' The temperature would rise and Vicente would say, 'There can only be one voice in training,' to which I would snap back I wanted a say too. This went on for some time in the early days and sometimes the argument would be carried over from the track to our relationship, but it was all part of adjusting to a very different regime.

Other athletes were also noticing a change in me away from the track. Sue Deaves, the England Team Manager, has told me that my reputation was as a very strict and disciplined athlete, someone for whom running was first, second and last. No one ever said this to my face but I began to hear from Paula that people were now saying that I seemed so much more relaxed. For one thing, I didn't talk about athletics all the time!

It was another change that took some time for me to adjust to. Vicente's attitude was that when you're on the track you treat it as your job, you do your work well and you come home to get away from it all and relax. It was hard for me to accept that he didn't want to come home from training and watch a video of the last European Championships. Initially I felt it showed that his dedication wasn't as strong as mine, but eventually I began to appreciate that there was life outside athletics. In the past I'd have felt terrible guilt pangs if I ate a bar of chocolate or lay in bed past eight o'clock (by that time I'd usually put in a training session before breakfast). Again, Vicente had a more laid back approach and would ask why I couldn't train whenever I woke up.

At the same time I was exploring a social life I'd never really let myself have before. In the past I'd only visited a cinema once or twice a year, but going to the movies was one of Vicente's passions, so we were soon queuing at the box office twice a week. I was training harder than ever before but also enjoying life more. I hadn't realised how hard I'd been on myself in the past, sacrificing everything to athletics. Having left my job at Ron Hill Sports the previous summer, I had time on my hands and soon discovered that being a full-time athlete wasn't enough to satisfy me. I started a part-time business and finance course at a local college and also made a brief entry into the world of modelling. The latter came about because I'd always had a keen interest in fashion. I often attended local fashion shows and even bought the odd designer outfit when money allowed. It was Vicente who suggested I ought to have a go at modelling myself. I went for an interview at Manchester Modelling Agency and was accepted for their free induction course.

The first day wasn't promising. I nearly abandoned the whole idea because I spent the whole time kicking my heels. We were choreographing a piece for a Christmas gala ball and my turn wasn't until scene twenty-two! In the end I persevered and learnt how to do quarter turns and full turns on the catwalk and how to apply make-up for the best results. We were taught dress and fashion sense, hygiene, cleanliness and book-keeping. I enjoyed it and made some great friends on the course.

The Christmas gala was great fun but I soon found out what real modelling was all about when I went for a casting. I was herded into a cramped room with other models who sat waiting for someone to flick through their portfolios for two minutes and say, 'Okay, you'll hear from us.' Later I did get an offer to do some modelling for a catalogue but by that time I had begun a university course and studying took up any time left over from athletics. Looking back, my modelling career never took off because I was unwilling to get on the phone every day and try to get myself into castings. I was an international athlete who'd travelled the world. I knew what I wanted and where I aimed to go, I didn't have the necessary desire to become a model.

If I saw a career for myself after athletics it was in the media. I was used to doing interviews after races and had appeared on *A Question of Sport*, *See Hear* (a magazine programme for the deaf) and numerous other programmes. I felt comfortable in front of the camera and had plenty of experience. However, media work was a competitive field and I realised that a qualification would be an advantage.

I applied to a course at Warrington, part of the University of Manchester, and was surprised and delighted to be accepted. I began a three-year degree course in the autumn of 1993. It was hard work in the first year, getting up early in the morning to train and then coming home after a full day's study to go running again. I worried at first that my studying might be affecting my athletics, but gradually I began to enjoy the course as a complete contrast from my other life. When I was at college I was a student and Diane Modahl the athlete was left at home. If anyone said, 'I saw you race on television last week,' I'd nod, but I wouldn't encourage the conversation to go on and never brought up the subject of athletics myself. College life was an escape that I would later grow to value more than I could have guessed.

Back on the track, the acid test for my new coaching regime was approaching. The 1993 World Championships in Stuttgart was our first major championship with Vicente in sole charge as my coach. I had raced well that season and everything was going according to plan, but could I reproduce the same form on the big occasion? Would my new training methods be vindicated or had I made a bad mistake?

As ever, we approached the World Championships with a target session that reproduced the same conditions – three hard races on consecutive days. On the first day of the target sessions I broke my personal best time. The second day also went well but by the end of the third I was absolutely exhausted. I felt disgruntled, where was the benefit in all this? I had finished the three days completely at rock bottom, which is the way you should never finish a training session. Vicente, on the other hand, was quite satisfied, he was adamant that we'd achieved everything we needed in preparation for Stuttgart. Time proved he was in a better position to judge than I.

On my first day at the World Championships I won my heat, coming in comfortably ahead of the field. The next day was semi-final day, the hurdle where in the past I had sometimes fallen against a world-class field. Vicente went over the race tactics with me time and time again. I was to stay close on the shoulder of the leader all the way, always alert for an attack at any time. I was a little dubious. In the past I had never stayed that close to the leaders in a world-class field because I hadn't the strength to maintain it to the finish. But he was the coach. I ran it the way we'd planned and felt so strong as we entered the final bend that I was even able to ease off towards the tape and qualify very easily.

I was in the final of the World Championships for the first time in my life. In 1988, when I'd reached the Olympic final at the age of 22, I felt that I'd already done all that was expected of me. I was so relaxed that I didn't do myself justice in the final. Stuttgart was different, I was a mature athlete of 27 with a coach who had prepared me specifically for the test I was facing.

We had a rest day before the final and left the village to relax as a normal married couple. I don't think we even discussed the next day as we both knew what I had to do. I was up against some impressive names: Maria Mutola and Tina Palino from Mozambique, Liliana Nurodinova, the defending world champion and the Romanian Ella Kovacs, to name a few. I knew who to look out for but the only thing that really mattered was Diane Modahl's race plan.

The gun fired and I got a reasonable position and held it as we went through the bell. With 300 metres to go I was feeling in great shape, totally concentrated and in control. This was the point where Mutola usually made her move and I was ready for it. She started to pull away and I went with her, so did the other front runners and there was the inevitable bump. I managed to keep my feet but it had disturbed all of us except Mutola who had a clear run to the finish. I was in third position and confident that I could still get a medal. But another vest went past me and, as we came to the line, I just couldn't close the gap.

I finished fourth in 1 minute 59.42 seconds. It was the highest position a British girl had ever come in the World Championships 800 metres and my best placing in a major event against a world-class field. There was a change in my form that was there for everyone to see. The commentators were saying, 'This is a different Diane Modahl, she is much tougher and finishing her races much stronger.'

If it hadn't been for the bump at the crucial stage of the race I might have come home with a World Championships medal. It would certainly have been close. What was in no doubt was that I'd had a year to be proud of. My new training regime was paying off handsomely. I had broken two minutes seven times that year, come second in the UK 400 metres Championships and finished fourth in the world in Stuttgart; 1993 was my most consistent year in athletics and there was every reason to look forward to the future.

Vicente and I celebrated the end of the season with a trip to Jamaica. Both our mothers came with us for the holiday. It was only the second time I had been back to my parents' birthplace and again we headed for the old house at the top of the hill where my grandmother lived. Vicente insisted that we drive there despite my mother's warnings that our hire car would never make it up the steep, narrow track. The locals were amazed to see a car begin the climb, engine revving and wheels spinning on the shingle. When the neighbours learnt that Miss Lena (my mother) and her daughter were inside, they congregated around the house, bringing armfuls of bananas as a welcome gift.

My grandmother had aged visibly since my last visit. Her hearing and eyesight were both failing but she knew me and recognised my husband from the photographs I'd sent. I showed Vicente my grandfather's grave in the garden and the place in the garden where my sisters and I had showered when I was 15. It was a unique moment in my life when three generations of my family were present together. Most parents take their children to see their grandparents when they are young, but for us Jamaica was thousands of miles away. It was the first time my mother, grandmother and I were together and, sadly, also the last. My grandmother was to die the following year, news that only reached me in the middle of the nightmare which began to unfold at the Victoria Commonwealth Games.

That year, 1994, should have been the one that marked the peak of my career. There was a triple crown of opportunities waiting for me in the European Championships, the Commonwealth Games, and the Europa Cup (with the prize of qualifying for the World Cup). It was a demanding season but Vicente and I had every reason to believe the year would bring greater honours than I'd ever won before. After the initial disagreements, we had settled into an excellent coach/athlete relationship. Any lingering doubts I had about Vicente's methods had been banished by the success at the World Championships the year before. This was to be our year, but instead it was the beginning of an ordeal that was worse than anything I'd ever faced in my life.

Early in the year I ran 2 minutes 2 seconds at the Indoor Games in Stockholm, confirming that everything was on course for the summer. Things only started to go wrong when we went to Mexico in April for altitude training. We stayed at the Hotel del Rey in Toluca, 2600 metres above sea level and only an hour's drive from Mexico City. Mexico held many good memories for Vicente as the place he had first met Said Aouita and begun their long association. What I will remember of Mexico that winter is lying in a bed with a fever and a severe throat infection.

The infection came out of the blue but refused to disappear as quickly. My throat was so sore that after two days I couldn't eat or speak. A Spanish doctor was called. Dr Llamas spoke a little English but Vicente was able to converse with him in Spanish. As always, Vicente took pains to explain that I was an athlete, so the doctor had to be very careful what he gave me. I couldn't take any anabolic steroids, synthetic steroids or dry stimulants as part of any medication. We always carried a list of what drugs were permissible. There were some things in the first prescription which were unacceptable. Vicente made that clear and the doctor suggested an alternative. I was given a throat spray and some pills. It was agonising to take them; my throat was so inflamed that I'd been spitting into a bowl to avoid swallowing.

The next day things were no better. My throat felt so raw that I couldn't even lay my neck on a pillow. I had to communicate with my husband by writing messages on pieces of paper. The Spanish doctor was called again. Vicente and I were both beginning to get anxious because I hadn't drunk or eaten anything for four days. This time the doctor suggested antibiotic injections and, by the following night, I had begun to show the first signs of recovery. The next day I managed to get up and walk. I was very eager to make up the week of training I'd lost but was forced to admit I needed more time to recover.

We returned to England the day after. Dr Llamas had left Vicente with another course of injections to give me. We never used them, waiting instead to see a doctor in England. Dr Milroy was a BAF medical officer used to dealing with athletes. He suggested that, in fact, I wasn't suffering from an infection but a very severe virus. The only remedy was rest and he advised us against continuing with the medicine I'd been given in Mexico as it was toxic and very strong. Did this episode have any bearing on the dope test I took some six weeks later in Portugal? I took a random drugs test shortly after my illness and that was negative, so the theory seems unlikely. However, medical experts have said it was theoretically possible that there might have been some reaction with the toxic medication that was still in my system some months later.

During the pre-season I felt an underlying tiredness whenever I raced or trained. Nevertheless by the summer I had recovered sufficiently to take part in the British AAA Championships in

Sheffield and win the 800 metres convincingly. We planned a trip to Portugal the following day to sharpen up for the Europa Cup in a warm climate. The race in Lisbon wasn't an important race on the calendar, it was just another race to use as a marker at the end of a hard training week. I thought nothing of going to Lisbon, how could I have known that I'd hear the name of that city over and over again in the future? Lisbon was the place my world started to fall apart.

Chapter 8

'Positive'

There were three reasons for Vicente and me to be in Lisbon in June 1994 – warm weather, good training facilities and a useful race to gauge my progress. The issue of dope taking in athletics didn't enter even remotely into my thinking. Yet on that day – 18 June – I am supposed to have taken a huge amount of testosterone at some point immediately before or after the race. (Medical experts later suggested within two hours before I took a drugs test.) Why should I have taken the absurdly dangerous risk of taking drugs on the day of a race and actually within the stadium? That was a question no one ever answered. It's well known that anyone wanting to cheat by using drugs does it during the winter months, in the build-up to the season. Anabolic steroids don't have any instant effect and would have to be taken over a long training period to produce any benefit. Yet I was tested four times between November 1993 and April 1994 and each time the result was negative. If I'd really had any intention of using drugs why would I have waited until the race season had begun, when there was least benefit and the greatest chance (bordering on certainty) of detection?

Leaving the crucial question of motive aside, I would have needed both the time and opportunity to take a massive dose of testosterone during the meeting at Lisbon. What follows is my own story of what happened that day. It was an account later submitted at my hearing. The details are nothing out of the ordinary, it was just another minor race in an athlete's season, but it must be asked, at what point did I find time and opportunity to commit the doping offence I was later charged with?

The race itself came the day after my twenty-eighth birthday, near the end of a hard training week. I was staying with Vicente and other British athletes at the Penta Hotel in Lisbon, which was also the headquarters of the Portuguese Athletics Federation for the meeting. At around 6.15 pm I left the hotel (1 hour 45 minutes before the race) and walked to the nearby track with David Grindley, the British 400 metres runner also managed by my husband. Vicente had already gone ahead of me because some of his other athletes were competing earlier.

David Grindley and I went straight to the warm-up area which by this time was busy with athletes preparing to run. I couldn't see Vicente so I sat down in the warm-up area to relax and read a book. Next to me was a Russian athlete who was also competing in the 800 metres. She sat with her coach. I watched a group of young boys playing football nearby. There were athletes, coaches and spectators in almost every part of the warm-up area, I was never alone at any time. I read my book, chatted to Vicente when he came over briefly, and then completed my own warm-up for around 45 minutes. David Grindley was later interviewed about the warm-up area himself and said, 'There were 200–300 people around at any one time . . . There wouldn't have been any chance for Diane to administer any banned substance without us noticing.'

Entering the stadium through the main entrance, I had about 15 minutes to go before the race. I joined the queue of athletes waiting for the toilet. It was very warm and I wore only a T-shirt and skin-tight track bottoms. I didn't take a bag or anything else into the toilet in which I could have concealed a syringe or tablets. In any case, there was the constant traffic of other athletes using the toilets before the racing began. As I came out, Suzanna Cabral and another Portuguese athlete were just ahead of me.

I went to the track where I was chaperoned to the start by an official, along with other athletes. The race itself was something of a disappointment. I ran my fastest time of the year but was beaten into second place by the Brazilian Mendes. I was annoyed with myself and knew I should have won. We were treating the race merely as part of a training camp so afterwards I wanted to cool down and get on with the rest of my training. Vicente and I went directly back to the warm-up area where we jogged for around ten minutes and I did some stretches.

While we waited by the tunnel for the award ceremony to be

announced I was approached by a race official who informed me
I'd been selected for random drug testing. (This happened about
twenty minutes after my race.) We went over to the prize-giving
area and hung around for some time with a lot of other athletes
before the presentation took place. I signed the form at 8.30 pm,
which meant we had an hour from that time before I needed to
go to the doping station. A random dope test was routine to me,
a procedure I'd been through countless times before. I knew well
that athletes who finish in the first three are especially likely to
be selected.

I told the official I wasn't yet ready to give a sample (athletes
are often dehydrated after a race). I still had more training to do
and the official said this was in order providing I didn't leave the
main arena where she could keep me under supervision. Since the
track events had finished I explained we'd be training on the main
track in full view of everyone. We did a short recovery session
where I ran four sets of 200 metres with Vicente timing me on
the stopwatch. I then took a ten-minute break sitting on the
infield, while I got ready for the next set. All this time there were
field events going on around me, other athletes were jogging and
warming down while spectators watched from the seating area.

After my recovery session I realised I only had around twenty
minutes before reporting to the doping control area. Vicente and
I went to find the official who had spoken to me before. She
was at the entrance tunnel which leads under the stadium to the
changing rooms. I asked if I should make my way over and she
asked me to wait there five minutes while she collected another
athlete. When she was ready, she escorted Vicente and me to the
doping control room.

When we arrived there were already two or three athletes
waiting to give a sample. Vicente and I had to wait outside in
the corridor. There were no chairs so we sat on the floor. I wasn't
ready to give a sample at that point anyway, so we were in no rush.
The sampling officers gave me a sealed bottle of water to drink
which I sipped outside in the corridor. Normally, there should
have been a security guard present to make sure that no one
wandered in and out (this is in International Olympic Committee
(IOC) regulations since dope tests are meant to be a highly secure
procedure). In fact there were no guards anywhere in evidence.

Finally we were allowed in to the doping control room, a small cramped area with an adjoining toilet and shower. There was already a Cuban athlete in there and one other girl sitting to our left. After all the waiting I was ready to give a sample but the official told me the girl sitting down was ahead of me in the queue. The Cuban athlete left to be replaced by two Kenyans; the room by this time was becoming quite crowded.

Having waited around half an hour in the room, it was finally my turn to give a urine sample. By then it was almost four hours since I'd left the hotel that morning. I chose a sealed plastic container and an 'A' and 'B' bottle for the sample to be divided between. (Two bottles are used so that if there is a positive test you have a second sample to confirm or deny the result.) When you give a sample for dope tests it is always supervised so the official who had brought me in was present all the time in the cubicle. I then carried the sample into the testing room to the doping officer. He did a pH test on the sample and wrote the figure 5 on the form (this was to be a critical point later). The sample was divided into the 'A' and 'B' bottles by the doping officer, who I later discovered was called Dr Pereira. Vicente and I were not entirely happy with the way the bottles were sealed. The tops were clicked into place and then just taped up with sellotape. This was a method I'd not seen for some time so we mentioned our concern to Dr Pereira. He said, 'That's okay because I'm going to seal it with wax. This is my personal seal. Don't worry, it can't be broken.' Wax was melted on the seal and then it was given an official stamp. We didn't make any further comment at the time. We'd watched the whole process closely and signed the form to say we were happy with the procedure.

That was the test over with. It had all taken around two hours from the time I was racing to the time I actually gave the sample in the doping control room. Within that two hour period after my race was the time I was supposed to have committed a drug offence. The dope test was something I'd been through so many times before. Time consuming, degrading, but necessary. I had no reason to believe that this test would be any different from all the others which had proved negative in the past. I went back to the hotel and thought no more about it. The day was 18 June 1994 – another nine and a half weeks would go by before I would be informed that my test had proved positive.

Back at the hotel that evening we celebrated my birthday

a day late, since there hadn't been much chance before the competition. Vicente had invited some of his athletes around with their families. The Castro twins, Domingos and Dionisio, brought a cake and some champagne and a number of friends gave me presents. It was a lovely end to a good week. Although the race had been a minor disappointment, it was a successful training camp all in all. I was already looking forward to the Europa Cup the following week. There was no sign, hint or warning that something had happened that week in Lisbon that would change my life out of all recognition.

The Europa Cup was held in Birmingham that summer. The top eight European nations were competing and we knew that the coveted prize at stake was a place in the World Cup finals at Crystal Palace. I had been selected to run the 800 metres for Britain in the Europa Cup on four previous occasions, never finishing higher than fourth. This time, running in front of my home crowd, was something special, all the more because my parents, my brother and my three recently adopted sisters were there supporting me.

I knew I would be up against some strong opposition from the East European runners but on my home turf I was prepared to take the race on. It was a damp windswept day and there was a long delay before the start because of a problem with the television coverage. Although it was June, the wind was so cold that I kept my T-shirt on until the last minute. When the gun finally fired, the race set off at a slow pace. That has the disadvantage of a lot of changing stride and bunching together, but I kept out at the front away from trouble. As we went through the bell, the French girl on my shoulder decided to wind up the pace. I was determined not to give up the lead so she had to run wide to try and pass me. Coming round the final bend we were neck and neck, both pushing for the line. But I was the stronger and crossed the line in front. I remember I was even able to save something in case an extra burst was needed at the last. It was a great feeling. The home crowd were roaring me on, my family jumping out of their seats, and I had won for the first time in the Europa Cup. It was my best race of the year and, as it turned out, the eight points I gained were vital to the British Women's team qualifying ahead of the Russians for the World Cup final. Those eight points were to cause more controversy throughout the international athletics world than any other in the history of the World Cup. By winning the race on 25 June I helped my country into the finals – two months later I found myself branded as the athlete who would get Britain thrown out of the competition.

I took part in other races that summer – the London Grand Prix and the Goodwill Games in Russia – but although I finished fourth in the latter, I wasn't feeling at peak fitness. I was finding training much harder and wrote in my diary that I felt tired and lethargic a lot of the time. Vicente maintained I was tired because I was training hard but when the lethargy failed to go away I was given an iron injection on 1 August by the BAF medical doctor, Patrick Milroy. I was unsure what was wrong – possibly I had over-trained or was still feeling the effects of a bug I'd picked up somewhere.

Nevertheless I was eagerly anticipating the two major events of the year: the European Championships and the Commonwealth Games. I'd broken two minutes at the Goodwill Games and finished fourth against the highest calibre field of the year. There was every reason to think I was in the form to challenge for medals at the big two competitions.

Yet August was the month when my season turned sour. My hopes at the European Championships were cruelly dashed by an accident that was beyond my control. The day was such a disaster that I have almost wiped it from memory and find it difficult to recall details of the race. I raced in the heats on 7 August, qualifying easily and feeling very much in control. The semi-finals took place the next evening and that was when the incident happened. Shortly after the race started we broke lanes at the 200 metres point and converged. As we all vied for a good position there were some collisions, several runners stumbled into each other and I came off the worst for it. A Russian athlete, Samarokova, an unknown at the time, pushed me from behind and I almost fell. I clutched at the girl in front to stop myself going down and managed to stay up on my knees. I hadn't hit the track but I was shaken and it was at this point that I probably made a mistake. Instead of sitting in the pack to recover and take a breather, I tried to make up the ground and push myself back to the front. I went straight from a bad stumble back into top gear and paid for it later. For the rest of the race I led until the final 100 metres but my concentration had been broken and it wasn't the way I'd planned to run. With a 100 metres to go the pace hotted up and I knew that I was in trouble. The reserve I normally relied on had been used up in that earlier burst of speed. When it came to the final kick for the tape I had nothing left to give.

It was a devastating defeat because my hopes had been so high. I walked off the track stunned and desperately upset; I'd lost the race on something that was beyond my control. I did make an official complaint but the jury decided it was an unfortunate incident and nobody was to blame. The girl who had pushed me was a very physical competitor and maybe a little inexperienced; she actually fell when it came to the final. I didn't really blame her or anyone else, it just felt an unfair way to go out of such an important championship.

I spent a day feeling very low and depressed. I had wanted to do well in the Championships so much and it was a shock to find myself dumped out at the semi-final stage. On 10 August, the day I should have been in the final, Vicente and I were out training instead. He could see my head was down and tried to encourage me.

'There is one way you can recoup the season,' he said, 'by winning the Commonwealth Games. You have to do that from today by getting your head together, because physically you're in great shape. I want you to go out today and just run. Train as though you're in the final.'

There were two major events that year, one had ended in disaster, now I had only the Commonwealth Games to set my sights on. At the time I thought my exit from the European Championships was the hardest blow of my career; I little knew that an ordeal was waiting two weeks later that would make it seem like a mere pinprick.

The next day I took the flight to Canada for the Games. They were to be held in Victoria, an island off the west coast of Canada, close to Vancouver. My first race wasn't until 24 August so I had almost two weeks to prepare myself and get into winning mode again. Vicente planned to fly over later in time to see the final. He had other competitions to attend in Zurich and Brussels where some of his other athletes were taking part.

Victoria was the smallest place ever to host a major Games. Its population is only a quarter of a million but what it lacks in size it makes up for in beauty. It is a city of parks and flowers, with large detached houses surrounded by beautifully kept gardens. There are lakes dotted around the island which reminded me of Norway.

I spent my time relaxing in the village with the other English athletes, including Paula who was there as usual to keep me company. I also went to some of the Bible studies and services organised by Christians in Sport. The services were an open door to anyone who wanted to attend. At one the long jumper, Yinka Idowa, stood up and talked about what her faith meant to her as an athlete and how she had become a Christian.

The days passed with training and telephone calls to Vicente. On 19 August I took part in a pre-Games meeting and ran 400 metres as a loosener to get my legs used to racing again after missing the European final. It was a boost to my confidence as I ran my second quickest time for that distance. I came home close to a girl who was a 400 metres specialist so I knew my speed was intact and I was in great shape. I wrote in my diary, 'I am confident to win, I'm strong to win, I'm determined to win.' That summed up my frame of mind. I was the Commonwealth 800 metres defending champion and I didn't intend to give up the title I had won in Auckland in 1990. I knew that the gold medal was there for me to claim if I ran my best race on the day. Then 24 August 1994 arrived, the day of the heats for the 800 metres and the day which was to be the most harrowing in my life.

I went out early, around eight o'clock in the morning, for a jog as I would on any other race day. I was wearing my jogging gear – a sweatshirt, lycra tights and a Nike cap on my head. Behind the village was a forest and I headed in that direction. It was a place of shadowy calm and quiet away from the buzz of the Games and the crowds of people. As I jogged through the wood it reminded me of Delamere Forest in Cheshire, a place where Vicente and I often went running together. My mind was on the race ahead and registering the way my body felt that morning. I felt a little bit lethargic but that wasn't a bad sign. It sometimes meant I'd had so many days' rest that I needed a really hard run to burn off the energy. The race was playing through my head like a video tape that kept rewinding. I saw myself arriving at the track, warming up, reporting, and heading towards the main arena. I knew what the plan was and I could picture myself taking up the position I wanted and moving through the stages of the race. On the day of an important race I am like most athletes, I develop a kind of tunnel vision that blocks out anything that might distract from the job in hand.

When I arrived back at the village I was going to take a shower and have breakfast. I had to pass the team manager's room – Sue Deaves' – and I was surprised when she appeared at the door and called me inside. It was a fairly small room like mine, with a bed on one side and a table where I could see official documents and race numbers stacked in neat, orderly piles.

She closed the door behind me and said, 'I think you should sit down.' I sat down on the bed, wondering what was coming. Sue held my hands and looked into my eyes. She was telling me she had some bad news. My first reaction was to think that there had been a death in my family. But after a pause of a few seconds which seemed like hours, she said, 'I've had a fax through from Peter Radford to say that the drug test carried out in Portugal has tested positive for testosterone . . .' There was another word but I didn't catch it.

At first I couldn't take it in. I wanted to leave the room to continue my routine of getting ready. I said, 'I have to go and prepare for my race now.'

'Oh no, I don't think that's best.'

I raised my voice impatiently, 'I have to. I'm racing in a few hours.'

Sue came close to me, took my hands and looked me in the eye. She spoke very firmly. 'No, Diane. I'm going to have to pull you out.'

That's when it hit me. Even though I'd been told about the drugs test, I still thought it was some terrible mistake that wouldn't affect my race. If I could just get back to my room and inside my tunnel vision this bad dream would melt away. But I wasn't going to be allowed to race. The impact of that began to sink in. Everything within me started to tear apart.

It is hard to explain what went through my head and what happened next in that room. I went into a state of profound shock and the events that followed became blurred and confusing. I was numb with disbelief. My legs and my whole body felt weak. It was difficult to get my breath. I felt hot and cold alternately. The room seemed unreal. It could not be happening, it wasn't happening.

At some point I found myself on the floor, although I didn't know how I came to be there. I was aware that Sue was slapping my face and saying, 'You must breathe. Breathe, Diane.'

It was only months later that she told us that I had actually passed out several times in the room. There was one point where I lay quite still with my eyes wide open and the pupils large and unmoving. Even when Sue passed her hand across my eyes they didn't flicker. She was scared. My hands felt cold and she said to herself, 'My goodness, she's dead.'

None of this I remember. I can only piece together the details from what others have said and the nightmarish fragments I can recall. I didn't have a clue why she was telling me to breathe. I thought I was all there. I remember standing up at one point and pacing feverishly around the room. I was looking out of the window where there was a grassy area full of trees. Earlier that week I'd stood there for the team photo to be taken. As I stared out I was banging on the wall, repeating, 'This is terrible. This is terrible.'

Sue was trying to calm me down, talking quietly and handling the situation as if she were my own mother. She was a pillar of strength and support. If she hadn't been with me I don't know whether I might have gone into a coma and never come round again. I started to ask for my training diary. I couldn't recall whether I'd been tested since Portugal. I was trying to remember the details of the procedure in Lisbon and whether they were correct. But it was difficult to think straight. Sue went to get my training diary and also decided to bring my Bible, maybe hoping it would calm me down.

It was the first time I'd been left in the room on my own. I suddenly felt completely and utterly alone. I went on my knees and started to pray with my elbows resting on the bed. It was a simple instinct. Something I'd done since I was a child. When Sue came back I was still in that position with my hands clasped. She put her hand on my shoulder and said, 'That's good, you pray.' I know that her faith was important to her too. Later she told us that events in that room disturbed her so much that she'd needed counselling to come to terms with it. She felt there was something wrong about it all. Athletes don't go into a state of profound shock, almost a coma, if they're being told about a drugs offence they know all about.

Alan Lindop (the British men's team manager) and Dr Roy Axon, the team doctor, arrived. Alan had brought the official fax which I'd asked to see. Sue Deaves suggested that Roy Axon read the fax to me. I stood beside him as he did so, just to make certain that there hadn't been some terrible mistake. The fax actually said my name – DIANE MODAHL. It was a shock to see it in writing. The letter was from the Portuguese Athletic Federation and was addressed to Peter Radford of the BAF. This is what it said (reproduced here without corrections).

Dear Sirs,
By the present we inform you that the results of doping control performed on Ms DIANE MODAHL, from Great Britain, in 'St Antonio Meeting' held in Lisbon on 18 June 94, according with the IAAF banned substances, have been positives. The report of the 'Doping and Biochemistry Analysis Laboratory' inform us that the Diane Modahl sample revealed TESTOSTERONE/EPITESTOSTERONE – equal to 42,08 – value to consider demonstrative of administration of TESTOS-TERONE exogenous.

We will attend for your contact in order to agree the date to conduct of the test on the reserve 'B' sample.

We obtained a copy of this fax later from the BAF. At the time I only took in my name and the words 'administration of TESTOSTERONE'. It gave me some grain of hope to cling on to: the idea that I had administered a drug was ridiculous, preposterous. It made me realise that some dreadful mistake had certainly been made. 'My God, my God, something terrible has happened!' I kept saying.

I must have collapsed again after the fax because the next thing I knew was that I was on the floor and concerned faces were peering down at me. I could hear Sue and Roy whispering to each other but couldn't catch what they were saying. The doctor pointed to his arm and I immediately feared they were going to give me an injection of some sort, perhaps to sedate me. I didn't want that, I wanted to be aware of what was happening. I tried to force myself to appear really awake and in control, although in fact I must have been quite hysterical. 'Pull yourself together, pull yourself together,' I was telling myself.

'Next thing you'll wake up to find yourself in a straitjacket or something.'

They didn't give me any sedation then. The doctor wanted me to lie flat on my back and put my legs up on a chair. He was treating me for shock although I couldn't even understand why he'd been called – I didn't realise I'd passed out several times. He asked me questions about how I was feeling and if I wanted some water. At one point he asked me if I'd taken drugs or anything illegal. 'Of course not!' I screamed angrily. He seemed embarrassed to have asked the question. I was becoming angry and hysterical again. It had taken some time for the truth to sink in that they actually weren't going to let me race. It was the 16th Commonwealth Games and I was here to defend my 800 metres title. Even with this terrible shock, my mind was still half focused on what I had to do that day. I found it unbelievable that I could actually be prevented from going out to the track. I started to insist on all kinds of things. I wanted to go back to my room. I wanted to talk to Vicente on the telephone. I wanted to talk to Paula. I wanted to talk to the whole world and *scream* my innocence.

Sue Deaves felt it would be better if we went to another room downstairs. She was probably worried that people would hear me raising my voice. Throughout the whole sad episode, Sue upheld her duty as team manager. In retrospect, I can see she had to think of the other athletes and how they might have been affected. There were other members of the team passing her room all the time. Paula Thomas was staying in the room opposite mine but Sue said it would be unfair for me to speak to her. She had already run in the 100 metres but was about to leave for the track and run the first round of the 200 metres.

We went downstairs to another room. On the way, we had to pass the athletes' common room. Roy Axon walked in front and Sue kept very closely behind me as we went down the stairs. I don't know if she feared I might collapse again or that I might try to run away. My Nike cap had fallen off while I'd been lying on the floor. She picked it up. 'Put your cap back on, Diane. Remember who you are, remember that there are other athletes around.'

I was chaperoned to the bedroom of Anne Hogbin, the general team manager of the English Commonwealth Games team. Vicente was phoned while I was present because I was still in such a state of shock that I couldn't dial the number myself. When he answered I found myself unable to speak, the words just wouldn't come out. I wanted to say, 'Help me'. 'Vicente, something terrible has happened.' My lips moved but no words came out of my mouth. I was just staring at the receiver. Finally Sue Deaves realised my distress and took the phone.

Vicente was at our house when the phone call from Victoria came. He had just been to the fish market in Sale to buy a trout and cook it, Norwegian style, for his lunch. The fish was sizzling in the frying pan and he was looking forward to it. He was in a good mood and singing to himself. In another day he anticipated flying out to Canada to watch me run in the final of the Commonwealth Games. The phone rang just as he sat down to eat.

When he picked up the receiver all he could hear was someone making sounds, as if they were in terrible pain and despair.

'Who is it? Who is it?' he asked, urgently.

There was a pause, then – 'Vince, Vince, can I speak to Vince?' said the voice on the other end.

He felt a wave of relief. Someone must have called a wrong number. Nobody called him Vince.

Then the caller asked, 'Can I speak to Vince Modahl?'

'Yes. This is Vicente.'

'I am Susan Deaves, I'm with the English team at the Commonwealth Games in Canada. I'm afraid I have some terrible news for you. Diane, your wife, has tested positive for testosterone at an athletics meeting in Lisbon last June. We are preparing for her to be sent home later today. We've had to pull her out of the race.'

Vicente was stunned. In the few seconds before the word drugs were mentioned his mind had been racing with every imaginable horror – maybe I'd been knocked down by a car or attacked by a maniac. But tested positive for drugs? It was too absurd to take in. He asked Sue to put me on the phone.

'Diane, it's me, I want my wife home,' he said. 'I want you home now, just come home. Remember we need each other so try to be strong on the way home and I'll be there to meet you in London. I just want my wife home.'

There were so many things he could have said. He might have said, 'This is insane, we'll fight it, Diane, we'll fight it all the way and get the best lawyers in the world.' But he didn't mention anything like that. He just said, 'I want my wife home.' Those were the words I so desperately needed to hear at the time. I was broken and lost, I needed something to hold on to.

I was finally able to get some words out, although they came falteringly. 'Vicente. It's terrible, they say I was tested positive for drugs in Lisbon. How can I have tested positive when I've never used drugs?'

'We'll have to find out what has happened later. First of all come home,' he repeated. 'I need you home.'

'I'm not allowed to defend my Commonwealth title. Why are they doing this to me?' I was almost whispering and couldn't find the words any longer. I broke down in tears. Sue Deaves took the phone. She promised to ring Vicente back later with details of how I was coming home and who would travel with me.

Much later, Vicente told me that, when he put the phone down, he'd gone into the hallway and taken down my Commonwealth Games gold medal from Auckland 1990. He held it in his hands and wanted to howl with pain and anger, instead all that came out was a hoarse cry. Both of us had now entered a hell of torment and we had no idea how we were going to survive it.

After the phone call, things started to happen very quickly in Victoria. They were phoning to try and get me a flight back to England that day. Meanwhile the doctor gave me half a Valium pill to take. It was the only medication I received, as I later refused to take any more Valium on the journey home.

A decision had to be made about how to break the news publicly. A discussion was going on around me about what should be said to the media. I was the subject but I felt like a helpless bystander, especially since the Valium was beginning to take effect. Sue Deaves said, 'We'll just say it like it is, that she's had a positive drugs test.' Caroline Searle, the press officer, shook her head. 'Absolutely not. We can't say that.'

'Well what can we say?'

'That she's got a stomach bug and we're sending her home.'

This was eventually agreed as the story. My only concern was that they didn't say that I'd tested positive for drugs because I knew it was untrue. The BAF and the England team management promised me that the media wouldn't be informed, everything would be okay and I would be sent home in secrecy. There

were three call-up times for the 800 metres and they decided
to delay the announcement right until the final call. Then the
commentators and the media would be told I'd been withdrawn
with a stomach bug. By delaying as long as possible, they hoped
to dampen any speculation from the press.

In fact, the reason given was changed. Vicente thought it
sounded very implausible. He told them that my grandmother
had died thirteen days ago (my parents had wanted to wait until
after I'd raced to tell me). It was eventually given out that Diane
Modahl had returned to England because of a bereavement in
her family.

I was told to lie down and rest. They wrapped me up warm
in a bed while Sue Deaves shuttled back and forth to my room,
packing my things. She lent me one of her own bags because she
didn't want to attract attention by carrying my suitcase down the
stairs. I asked for my Bible and started to read, hoping to find
something that would comfort or speak to me. By this stage the
Valium had started to make the world move in slow motion, it
was hard to concentrate.

I asked Sue, 'Why has this happened? Why? I understand
that maybe I became too channelled in my athletics, too single-
minded, and I was forgetting about my faith. Perhaps that's why
God punished me by having such a disaster at the European
Championships.' It was my way of trying to find some logic
in it all.

Sue said, 'Yes, you might be right. Maybe you became too
selfish. God might look at it that way.' She went on to tell me
about a sad personal event in her life when she herself had found
comfort in God. Then we said a prayer together and she left me
reading and holding on to my Bible.

A flight home was booked for 5.30 pm that afternoon. I
locked the door and had a shower. People had been following
me everywhere since my ordeal started and I just wanted some
time alone. Even then Sue would knock on the door every few
minutes to check if I was all right. She was obviously so worried
that she didn't want to let me out of her sight.

Later the taxi drew up right outside the door. A nurse had been
sent to accompany me on the journey home. She didn't have any
idea what it was all about but Vicente had insisted I shouldn't be
sent back alone. He was deeply concerned about the state I was

in. Sue Deaves met the nurse at the village and explained only that I was ill and being sent home; I would need supervision on the journey.

I got into the taxi and we drove off. I could see the village disappearing past the windows. There was the spot where I'd posed in a team photo a few days ago. At eight o'clock that morning I'd gone out the door, ready and eager to run my race and defend my Commonwealth title. Nine hours later, I was in a taxi being smuggled in secrecy out of the village to be sent home. It was impossible to take in. The shock was so great that I was almost past caring by that stage. I was just letting things happen around me. They could have driven off and put me on a plane to the North Pole and I wouldn't have known the difference. All that I could keep in my mind now was to get home to my husband. To be with Vicente and let him hold me in his arms.

The nurse was trying to be pleasantly talkative in the back of the taxi, asking if I'd seen much of Victoria on my stay. I gave one-word answers. I wasn't in the mood to hold a polite conversation. The Valium hadn't sent me to sleep but I felt shut in my own world, numb to all the sights and sounds outside. We were taken first to the hospital to collect another athlete. Paul Edwards, the 34-year-old shot putter, was sent home on the same plane as me. His circumstances were very different from mine. He'd been in hospital with a blocked intestine since arriving in Canada and wasn't fit to compete.

I didn't know Paul Edwards personally. All I knew was that there were rumours about his involvement with drugs even before the Games opened in Victoria. Only the previous night, I'd been discussing it over the evening meal with some other English athletes including Paula Thomas, Linford Christie and Gowry Retchekan. Having heard that he was severely ill in hospital, we'd sent Paul Edwards a 'Get well' card from the whole team. Now the rumour was going round that he'd tested positive for drugs. I commented that I never would have signed the card if I knew he'd tested positive. Some of the others thought this was a bit hard. 'The guy's ill! Have some mercy!' they said.

I didn't think he deserved it. My feelings about drugs in sport had always been that strong and clear cut. You shouldn't be taking them and if you got caught you deserved what you got. Nobody seemed very shocked or surprised about Edwards.

Linford Christie was saying, 'You have to be so careful now. You just don't know what's going on. Rumours are flying left, right and centre.'

One rumour going round was that another British athlete had tested positive. Gowry Retchekan asked, 'Is there any truth in it?'

'Apparently it was somebody who was at the European Championships,' Linford replied. I don't know where that rumour came from but somebody must have started it. It was so ironic that I was taking part in a conversation that was actually about *me*, without ever suspecting it. The idea that I could be the British athlete who was supposed to have tested positive just didn't enter my head.

We transferred to an ambulance at the hospital. Paul Edwards was on a stretcher, and had to remain lying or sitting down for the whole journey home. I later learnt that he'd tested positive at the European Championships and was also randomly tested on several occasions before the Games started.

There were five of us, the doctor driving, two nurses, myself and Paul Edwards. Since Victoria was an island we first had to get the ferry to Vancouver where the main airport was located. The medical staff were under strict instructions that they mustn't stop anywhere or talk to anyone, because we didn't want to attract attention from the media. I'd been up since eight o'clock that morning and had eaten nothing since my ordeal had begun. By this time it was well into the afternoon.

The long journey home began. We were given a private room on the ferry. Paul Edwards had to lie down on a couch. I wanted to get away to be on my own so I went for a walk up on deck. I leaned on the hand rail, watching the waves in the grey-green, impassive sea. I felt I was in the wrong place at the wrong time. What was I doing on this boat heading home for England when I should have been back in Victoria running the race of my life? I was trying to gather my thoughts and hold on to reality but everything seemed alien and distant. It had all taken place so quickly – in the space of a few hours. I couldn't believe that what I'd been through that day was really happening to me, Diane Modahl. It made no sense, no sense at all.

A short while later we were sitting on the plane that would deposit me back in England. Our seats had been booked in business class. Under normal circumstances I might have been delighted to travel in such comfortable surroundings, but this wasn't normality and I hardly noticed anything around me. I sat in a two-seater, next to a stranger, locked in my own world. Paul Edwards sat next to the nurse who was accompanying us to England. Conversation was almost non-existent on the journey. I didn't watch any films, didn't read, write, listen to music or eat. Although the Valium had made the world slow down, I couldn't sleep. I thought about one thing only. Seeing Vicente. I'd been told that on arrival they'd take us to a hospital in Northwick Park on the outskirts of London. I had no idea why I was being taken there but Vicente had promised to be there when I arrived. I desperately needed to see him again. It was the only thing left that I could see clearly.

After a journey that seemed to go on for a lifetime, the captain's voice asked us to fasten our safety belts, we were coming in to land at Heathrow. Home. To be with my husband, see Vicente. But home to what else? I really had no idea what to expect. Last time I had come home from the Commonwealth Games there had been a crowd of reporters and photographers waiting on the tarmac. Three of us had returned from Auckland with medals and mine was the only gold. I was proud of what I'd achieved. It was the greatest moment of my athletics career so naturally I was happy for the papers to be there to record the occasion.

This time was different. I just wanted to be left alone. The security around our return had worked well up to this point, there had been no reporters or prying cameras in Vancouver. But what would be the scene waiting for us in London? They had promised me that there would be no leaks to the press. I hoped the promise had been kept. As soon as I stepped off the plane I knew differently. The media storm had broken – and I was at the centre of it.

Chapter 9

Fighting Back

Our arrival at Heathrow was covered by every national newspaper and made the leading story on the six o'clock news that evening. I don't know what I had expected but I couldn't have prepared myself for the barrage of television and press cameras that met us. The ambulance sat at the main entrance for what seemed like an eternity while they picked up our luggage. There were lenses pushed up against every window, front and back. We were trapped like animals in a cage. Paul Edwards was getting more and more wound up. 'I'm going to punch one of these guys in a minute,' he growled.

As we drove away in the ambulance all I could think of was that very soon I'd see Vicente at Northwick Park. I hadn't spoken to anyone for a long time but now I kept asking the driver, 'How long will it take? How close are we?' The journey through North London seemed endless. Every few minutes we glanced anxiously behind to see if any of the press were following us. Edwards asked the driver if it had been in the papers. 'Yes, it's all over the papers. You've been on the news every five minutes in a bulletin.'

I was astonished. I'd done nothing wrong so I'd no reason to arrive home in secret but I hadn't been prepared for this media frenzy. Sue Deaves and Caroline Searle had been strenuous in stressing that the press wouldn't know anything before I left. He I was, just set foot back in England and already the story was blazed across every newspaper headline. How could they have known so soon?

The ambulance finally pulled into the forecourt of the Northwick Park Hospital in Harrow. It was the hospital used by the British Olympic Association for athletes, but I still wasn't sure why I'd been brought there. The ambulance door was opened and I climbed out. When the door was shut, someone was standing behind it. It was Vicente, holding a bunch of red roses. Flowers were the last thing I was expecting, but they were so typical of him. We didn't need to say anything. We just embraced and held each other. It was the only good moment of the last twenty-four hours. At least we were together again. Whatever we were going to face – and we had little idea then – we would face it together.

We were shown to a room and had some time alone. Ten minutes later Paul Edwards was wheeled in and we moved to an office belonging to a Dr Harris, which was the name of the doctor Vicente had been given. While we were alone we began to talk about the ordeal we'd been through. I wanted to know everything from Vicente – who he had spoken to, what he'd heard and why we'd been brought to this place.

Vicente told me that Caroline Searle, the press officer, had telephoned him from Victoria just before they announced that I wasn't going to race. She said that rumours had reached the press and warned him to travel to London before reporters started to lay siege to our house in Sale. The last thing he did before leaving was to turn on the television set to see the semi-finals of the Commonwealth Games 800 metres. Maybe it was all a bad dream and I would be there on the starting line, where I should have been. All the names of the runners came up on the screen. His heart leapt as he saw my name, Diane Modahl. Then he saw the letters next to it: NS – not starting. Vicente felt sick inside and switched off the set.

The phone rang before he could leave. 'Hello I am calling from Victoria, Canada. I work for the *Daily Mail*. We've just been informed that Diane will not be defending her title and is travelling home due to a family bereavement. Is that true?'

'Yes, that's correct. Her grandmother has died.'

'Rumours say that the real reason is because she's tested positive for drugs. Have you any comments?'

'No comments.' Vicente hung up and left. The siege had started. Our lives were no longer our own private affair. He packed clothes for both of us. We didn't even know if we would be able to return to our own house.

There had been other phone calls. On the journey to London, Vicente got a call from a fellow athletics manager, John Bicourt.

'What in God's name is going on?' he asked. 'What has happened to your family? Is there anything I can do?' As Vicente started to explain the whole sad saga, its impact had hit him again. He broke down and had to pull over to the hard shoulder. John Bicourt recommended his lawyer, Tony Morton-Hooper, who knew the IAAF well and was at the time representing the Kenyan athlete John Ngugi. Tony was on the phone before Vicente had reached Birmingham – he was to become our greatest ally in the weeks ahead. We had someone who was willing to take up our case. It was the first move towards fighting back.

Another call came from Vicente's secretary, Lesley Pilkington. She was holding the fort at the house, answering any calls that came in for Vicente in his office. Lesley said that our whole street was covered by the press – newspaper reporters, television crews, local and national radio – they were all camped outside the gate. Lesley had only taken on the job as Vicente's secretary some weeks before; she little knew what she'd let herself in for. Over the next six months she was another tremendous pillar of support in the fight to clear my name.

As to why the two of us were sitting in a doctor's office in Northwick Park Hospital, Vicente knew no more than I did. He was concerned that they might be planning to open the 'B' test – the second sample that would confirm or deny the 'positive' result. We didn't want that to happen until we'd found some medical experts of our own to be present. The opening of the 'B' sample was crucial to our case. In the end, we put an end to the speculation by asking for Dr Harris. When he arrived we were surprised that he had no answers to our questions. Perhaps, he suggested, we had been brought there to hide us from the press and to see if any medical help was needed. It seemed it was just a convenient place to take us from the airport. I assured him that I was ready to leave, I would be okay with Vicente.

A few minutes later we were on our own. Quite literally. We put my luggage in the boot of our black BMW, closed the doors and drove away. We felt conflicting emotions – relief and fear. We were jubilant to be back together, but the truth was dawning on us that we were now cast adrift; just Vicente and I driving through London with no idea where to go or what to do. We had left behind Victoria, the English team management, the media, and the hospital. It was now just the two of us – against the world.

While I was arriving back in London, the news had been broken to the English athletes back in Victoria. I learned the story from Paula Thomas later. It seemed that when I was in Sue Deaves' room, I must have been making more of a commotion than I realised. The girls rooming next door heard it and recognised my voice. One of them actually told Paula, 'I think something's happened to Diane.' Paula had then gone to the track to race but thought it very strange that I wasn't there to watch her. Normally I would have waited after my race to walk back with her.

She had heard rumours that I'd been sent home because my grandmother had died or because I was sick; there were different stories going round, but none of them set her mind at rest. In the end she went to Sue Deaves and demanded to know what was going on. Sue was tight-lipped. She was under strict orders from the BAF not to say anything to anyone. No matter how Paula argued and demanded, Sue Deaves would give no information about me.

By late in the evening the rumour was out that I had been sent home because of allegations that I'd tested positive for drugs. Somebody said there was going to be an announcement on television, although no names would be mentioned. Many of the women's team sat in the common room to watch, along with some of the male athletes who'd also heard the rumour. Past midnight the BBC news was relayed, via satellite, to Victoria. They said that two British athletes had been sent home because of drug taking and they named Paul Edwards and myself. The atmosphere in the common room was one of pure shock and disbelief. Some athletes were so deeply upset that it was impossible to consider going to bed. Sue Deaves was found and some of the girls insisted that she explain exactly what had happened. Although it meant going against her orders from the BAF, Sue sat down and told them what she knew.

The girls weren't willing to let it rest there. They all knew me and were sure that I wouldn't have anything to do with taking drugs. They got the team doctor, Dr Milroy, out of bed and insisted on speaking to him. Paula said, 'I don't know if I'm breaking a promise here between friends, but I feel that I know Diane well enough to say that she did find a lump in her breast earlier in the summer. I want to know if that could have had a connection?' The doctor was sorry. He didn't know the case personally and couldn't say if there was any connection. He said he was just as shocked as they were. None of the girls was able to sleep that night and Sue Deaves later told us that the shock certainly affected some members of the team badly.

Back in London, Vicente and I decided to spend the night in a hotel while we thought what to do. We knew we couldn't go home because our house was still besieged by an army of reporters. I was hungry so we stopped at a fish and chip shop near Harrow. It had a small area with tables and chairs where we sat down to eat. As we looked around we began to notice the morning newspapers that several customers were reading. The story, with my picture, was on every front page. Vicente was looking uncomfortably at the floor. I said, 'Don't look down, because I've done nothing wrong. Try to be natural.'

'It's not so easy,' he said. 'I've never been in the situation before where my wife is on the front page accused of something as terrible as this.' It seemed there was no escaping.

We drove to a Holiday Inn, just off the M1, and checked into a room. We arrived around 11 am and stayed in our room for virtually the next twenty-four hours. The day-time was spent talking on the phone and to each other. The night-time we tried our best to sleep. Vicente kept his arms around me. He told me that several times during the night I started to shake quite badly. There were distressed phone calls from athletes and friends in Victoria. Kevin McKay, who was best man at our wedding, was emotionally shattered by the news. He was a medal contender in the 1500 metres final, but athletics now seemed irrelevant to him.

'How can I concentrate on running?' he asked Vicente. 'I'm physically fit but mentally I've got nothing left. It's every athlete's nightmare and I know Diane is innocent. Everybody over here is in shock. It's all over the news, the press are going crazy and we all feel totally disgusted.'

When Vicente talked to Tony Morton-Hooper, the lawyer taking up our case, I would sit close and listen to the receiver. I still wasn't in any state to discuss the situation. Vicente would do the talking and I would ask questions or make suggestions through him. That was the way it operated from the start.

We left London in the morning and started to begin the long journey north. We were just driving because we still hadn't any definite plan of where to go. Our own home was barred to us, even my parents' house wasn't safe because the press were bound to come looking there. In the end we decided the safest refuge, and the place where we'd feel most comfortable, was at my sister Barbara's house. Barbara lived with her 8-year-old daughter in a two-bedroom house in Manchester. She welcomed us to come even though it meant giving up her own bedroom.

All the way to her door we were looking anxiously over our shoulders to make sure we weren't being followed. It was as if we'd become fugitives in our own city. Barbara met us at the door and we hugged and cried. Once inside, my family were soon on the phone wanting to know if we were all right. My father was utterly distressed by what had happened, he was alone since my mother was away in Jamaica and no one had been able to contact her. I told him that I didn't want her to know because her own mother had just died (Vicente had told me the news at the hospital). I didn't want her to rush home and miss the burial because of me.

We stayed at my sister's house for around two weeks and during that time a lot happened. We kept away from our own house. Lesley would make secret trips over to see us, bringing faxes and messages. She had to make sure the reporters outside wouldn't follow her so she would breeze out to her car, calling, 'I'm just going out to the chippy to get some lunch, you can follow me if you like!'

From the first day, letters of support started to pour in from athletes, friends and complete strangers all over Britain. They meant a great deal, especially in those early days. Although we were both feeling fragile and shell shocked, we knew we had to try and get ourselves into fighting mode. No one else was working to prove my innocence. We were completely on our own. From the day I flew out of Vancouver, the British Athletic Federation washed their hands of me. I had been running to represent my country since the age of 17, I was a valued member of the British Women's Team, in Auckland I did a lap of honour holding the Union Jack, yet now it seemed I was abandoned, an outcast. When I arrived back from Victoria there was no one there to meet me. It took a long time for it to dawn on me that no help, support or encouragement would come my way from the BAF.

The first step in our fight was to meet our lawyer, Tony

Morton-Hooper. He had actually cut short his holiday on the south coast to answer our call for help. He was our lifeline, our one hope, and I wanted to make a good impression on him when we first met. Even though I felt I was crumbling away inside, I wanted to prove to him that I was innocent and determined to clear my name. He didn't know me; all he would have seen was the TV image they replayed over and over again of me leaving the plane, looking dazed and shell shocked.

We felt confident in Tony as soon as we met him. He was relaxed and casually dressed but when we got down to business, he knew how to set about building a case. The first step was for me to make a detailed statement right away, while it was all fresh in my mind. Especially he wanted to know everything that had happened in Lisbon when I'd given the sample.

All that week, the Commonwealth Games was going on with the pictures relayed to us via the television. Events on the track were being overshadowed by the speculation surrounding my case. It seemed that everyone had a right to say what they thought about me. One night at Barbara's I listened to Brendan Foster saying how awful it must be for the members of Sale Harriers where I'd been a member since a teenager. How terrible for children in the primary section to hear all this happening. I felt he was implying that I'd brought shame and disgrace on my club. I thought, 'How can he say that? He doesn't even know what's happened!' I was so incensed that I actually phoned Caroline Searle in Canada and asked her to tell Brendan that he had no right to say such things.

Athletes who knew me were starting to speak out in my defence. One night we watched a live link-up with Linford Christie talking to Desmond Lynam. Linford made it quite plain he couldn't believe I was someone who'd take drugs. He believed I was innocent and the mistake was with the system. Vicente and I had tears rolling down our faces as we watched the screen; he was supporting us publicly on national television. David Grindley and John Regis added their voices to the growing number in my defence. Tony Jarrett said that if I had that amount of testosterone in my body I'd have a beard like Barry White!

People probably wondered why I didn't speak out myself. Every day my name was in the papers and it was incredibly frustrating not to be able to answer back. I wanted to say, 'Slow down. I am innocent. I've done nothing wrong, this is all ridiculous.' But the truth was, I felt in no fit state to string two words together. The shock and trauma affected me deeply. I was ill for three days on my return home to England. Tony, in any case, advised me to let other people do the speaking for me. 'You don't need to say a thing at the moment,' he said. 'To be honest I just don't think you would do yourself justice right now.'

After the three days when I was too ill to do anything, I went back to my daily training routine. Despite what I'd been through, I was still an athlete and I hadn't given up any of my ambition to be one of the best in the world. I wasn't about to quit because I had been falsely accused of taking performance enhancing drugs. Yet I couldn't help noticing a difference when I went running. Nothing felt right. The Commonwealth Games was going on in Victoria so what was I doing pounding away in a Manchester park? I found I was running as a release, to channel some of the pain and anger that was burning inside me. Often I would run very fast until I felt pain in my legs and chest. I would push myself to my limit quite deliberately, wanting it to hurt. Vicente came with me on these sessions and would complain that he couldn't keep up with me. I would set off as if I was running for my life, and keep going round and round until I reached the point of exhaustion and lay down in a sweating heap. It wasn't about pleasure any more, it was an act of defiance. Whatever they'd done to me, no one could take this away. Those sessions seemed destructive on the surface, but afterwards it felt good because some of the anger and frustration had been burned off with the energy.

While Vicente spent hours on the phone – to Tony, the BAF, and answering constant calls from journalists – I was running and writing. Tony wanted me to remember everything in detail so I began to write down what had happened. As the weeks went by both Vicente and I started to keep a personal diary of what we were going through. We had no thoughts about publication, we just needed to get our feelings down on paper as a means of survival. The pain of each day was too much to bear without some way of channelling it outside ourselves and trying to understand what it all meant.

There was plenty to write about. The date for the opening of the 'B' sample had been set for Monday, 29 August at 4 pm. Istvan Gyulai, General Secretary of the IAAF, gave us this staggering piece of information through our lawyer. Every athlete has the right to be present at the opening of a 'B' sample, since it provides the vital confirmation or denial of a positive test. In our case we were told the date on Saturday, giving us just two days' notice to be in Lisbon. If we weren't there, the 'B' sample would be opened regardless and our rights would be waived. It was a cruel slap in the face for us. I had only been back in England three days. How were we supposed to gather our medical experts, look at all the evidence and be in Lisbon for 29 August? We hadn't even received the chain of custody papers to show that the samples had been treated with the proper security since June. Vicente was so angry that he telephoned Istvan Gyulai at the IAAF.

He said, 'How is it possible to say that two days from now we are going to meet in Portugal to open a "B" test. We must have more time, we must receive the proper documentation and be able to read it through with medical experts. Then we can open the "B" test.'

Gyulai replied it was out of the question. There was a World Cup in England coming up in ten days' time and my case had to be out of the way. Either we were there at 4 o'clock, Monday afternoon, or I waived my rights to be represented. The only offer he was prepared to make was that the 'B' sample could be delayed until Wednesday – if we agreed to the hearing being held *the very next day*. We knew what that meant, innocent or not I would be found guilty because we'd have no time to prepare a defence.

The IAAF held all the cards and we had no choice. It was a case of be there or be damned. I wasn't easily shocked any more. We were being pushed up against a wall and there was nothing we could do about it. In the end we decided Vicente would make the trip on Monday morning. I was in no shape to face another media bombardment – and the trip was bound to be the focus of intense publicity.

Considering the pressure, I had managed to stay relatively calm most of the time, but there were occasions when my patience gave way under the strain. On one such day we came home to get some clothes. We were still staying at Barbara's house and I hadn't set foot in my own house for almost a month. I was upstairs in the bedroom when the injustice of it all came home to me with its full force. There I was, packing a bag to leave again, I couldn't live a normal life, people were calling me a cheat, I'd been forced out of my own home and all the time I felt I ought to be in Canada taking part in the Commonwealth Games. Something snapped within me. I picked up the nearest thing, which happened to be the remote control for the hi-fi, and threw it with all my strength at the door. It shattered into tiny pieces. I started to sweep other things off the shelf and on to the carpet in a blind rage. Vicente had to grab me and hold me on the bed till I calmed down, to stop me doing any more damage.

It wasn't the first or the last time that I had such an outburst. Nobody – not even my husband – could fully know what I was enduring. I felt like a prisoner. Everyone was so concerned about my health and my state of mind that I couldn't be left alone. It was almost as if there had to be a twenty-four hour vigil to keep me company. It had started from the moment I'd been told the news in Victoria and continued until Vicente went to Lisbon.

On the morning I dropped him at the airport I decided I'd had enough. I came home and went for one of my maniac runs. When I returned Barbara had gone to work so I had a bath, put on a nice dress and went out shopping. It was another small act of defiance. I knew my picture was on the television every day and I risked being recognised, but so what if people did look at me? I'd done nothing that meant I had to hide myself away. I walked around Habitat, looking at the furniture and then took myself out to lunch at a Spanish restaurant in Didsbury. Whilst I was there I wrote five or six more pages of my diary.

It was the first time I'd been alone since the whole ordeal had started. When I got home there were a string of messages on the answerphone. Nobody knew where I'd gone, they were all worried that I might have run off and done something silly. I'm the youngest – the baby of our family – and my brothers and sisters naturally felt protective towards me. But I was a mature, independent woman with a brain I could use, I wanted to be able to make my own decisions. If I wanted to scream, then I'd scream, if I wanted to stroll around a shopping centre like a normal person then I would. I needed some space and air to breathe. I knew they all meant well, but I was suffocating from kindness.

Vicente meanwhile was on his way to Lisbon, the city where all our troubles had begun. He was accompanied by two of our medical experts, Dr Malcolm Brown, who is the head medical officer for the British athletics team, and Professor Arnold

Beckett, one of the founders of 'Doping Tests in Sport'. In Lisbon they would meet up with Professor Peter Radford and Dr Cowan, there to represent the British Athletics Federation.

Arriving at Lisbon airport, they faced their first hurdle – a mass of press, TV and radio reporters waiting for them at the Arrivals point. Luckily, the press were all expecting to see me, so no one paid much attention as my husband and two doctors changed some money and walked straight past. Once outside, they joined the queue for a taxi, joking about how easily they'd been able to give the reporters the slip. Their luck didn't last, however: a reporter from the *Manchester Evening News* spotted Vicente and suddenly the chase was on. Through the glass they could see around forty reporters stampeding towards the double doors armed with cameras and microphones. In a few seconds they were surrounded. 'Is Diane guilty?' 'What do you expect of the "B" test?' 'Do you think there is a conspiracy against you?' Questions flew through the air as they struggled to force their way into a taxi.

I saw the pictures later on the evening news. It was hard to watch. My husband looked pale, ill and desolate. He answered one question and I could hear the edge of anger in his voice. It wasn't like him at all.

Throughout the trip I kept in contact with Vicente on his mobile phone so that he could tell me any news as it developed. Sometimes he sounded hopeful, sometimes not. Mostly we both felt sad because he should never have needed to go there in the first place.

We had been told the 'B' sample would be opened at 4 o'clock that afternoon. But when Vicente and the others arrived at the address of the accredited laboratory, they were informed it was closed for renovation. The security guard informed them that the operating laboratory had moved to the Instituto Medicina Legal, actually within the city mortuary. Vicente then asked if they could see Dr Barbosa, the official who had supervised my test. The guard phoned the laboratory and came back to say Dr Barbosa was on holiday. He would be available at 9.30 the next morning when the 'B' sample would be opened. Vicente and the others all felt angry. They had been pressurised into coming by the IAAF and now it turned out they'd been given the wrong address, the wrong day, and the doctor himself wasn't even there to meet them. Didn't anyone know they were coming?

They decided to investigate the new laboratory anyway. Arriving in a taxi, Vicente first wanted to see what the security was like for himself. He walked in the entrance and passed a receptionist reading a magazine, there was no security guard or anyone to challenge him. He walked right through the reception area, came back and had to make a noise before the receptionist could drag herself away from her magazine. The others then came in and one of the laboratory staff coming downstairs recognised Professor Beckett, who is a highly respected figure in the world of dope testing. They asked if Dr Barbosa was there.

'Oh yes, he's upstairs.'

Vicente and the others exchanged surprised glances. What was going on? They went up to the third floor and found Dr Barbosa at his desk. Again there was no evidence of any security and the doors to the laboratories were wide open. Dr Barbosa regretted that he couldn't give them the analytical report on the 'A' sample. He would bring it to them later at their hotel. It was yet another frustrating evasion and delay.

When Vicente spoke to me later that evening I was full of questions but there were no answers. He sounded tired and emotionally drained. All day they had been given the run around and got nowhere. This time it was my turn to give him the support he needed. The following day we would finally know the result of the 'B' test.

Next morning Vicente confessed to Malcolm Brown he felt scared and sick. It was a situation he had never expected to face in his life. He had always been honest and so had I. What happened if the 'B' test confirmed the 'A' test? It was unknown in the history of dope testing for one to contradict the other.

Malcolm was reassuring. 'It's normal to be scared and you have to expect a positive 'B' test. It doesn't mean that Diane used drugs, we both know she didn't. There are a lot of questions that still need to be answered.'

They joined Dr Cowan, Professor Beckett and Peter Radford at breakfast. The conversation turned away from my case to the general topic of drug testing in sport. Somebody cracked a joke which made the others laugh. Vicente thought, 'For them it's just a case, but for us it's the gravest day of our lives.' He looked down at his breakfast, struggling to keep his tears under control. The emotional strain of the day was already unbearable. Excusing himself hurriedly, he left the table and sought a quiet corner in the reception area. There he sat down and abandoned himself to the heaving sobs that shook his whole body. When he returned to the breakfast table, the conversation had gone quiet and there were no more jokes.

At 9 am the day's events began to unfold. A car arrived at the hotel for the BAF representatives but there was no car provided for Vicente or our two witnesses. It was yet another example of Portuguese efficiency. Fifteen minutes later they arrived at the Instituto Medicina Legal. Its location within the city mortuary seemed grimly appropriate to Vicente's mood. The cameras were waiting outside and again it was a battle to wade through the sea of journalists. The five of them were shown into Dr Barbosa's office where various officials were waiting. In addition to Dr Barbosa, there was Professor Les Reys (scientific Director of LADB, the lab), Mr Mota and Mr Salcedo, President and Vice President of the Portuguese Athletic Federation, and Dr Dolle of the IAAF Doping Commission. A meeting was held to discuss the plan of action. When our side asked for the chain of custody papers – which show where the samples were kept and when they were moved – they were told the documents weren't available. They reluctantly agreed to go ahead on the promise that the papers were in order and would be handed over during the day.

The 'B' test was produced, opened and taken away for analysis. Only Dr Barbosa, Dr Cowan, Professor Beckett and Dr Dolle were present for the tests.

Vicente was a prisoner inside the building while the long, tortuous wait begun. Outside, the press had surrounded the doors, making it impossible to go out. He decided to pass the time by calling Brendan Pittaway, who was doing his own investigation of my case.

In the week that followed my return from the Commonwealth Games it sometimes felt like we had every journalist in Britain trying to contact us. Yet one stood out from the rest for his sheer persistence. Brendan Pittaway, a journalist with BBC North West, called every day and several times a day. His messages were always the same – that he wanted to work with us so that my innocence could be proved. After the things that had been written about me in some papers I wasn't eager to trust any journalist. Vicente, however, argued that it would be useful to have an ally who could do some investigation on their own account. Brendan seemed genuinely concerned that an innocent person had been found guilty, so we eventually agreed to work with him. The arrangement was that we would supply Brendan with names and addresses, but would take no part ourselves in any investigation – that was entirely up to the BBC. One of the questions we wanted answering was, how did the Russians learn that a British athlete had tested positive in early July when I only learnt the news myself on 24 August, six or seven weeks later?

When Vicente called Brendan from the Lisbon laboratory, the journalist had hard evidence to confirm this. He read an article printed in the *Moscow Sport Express* on 9 July:

A British female athlete has failed a drugs test and so the Russian team, which the British beat by one point, will now qualify for the World Cup final at Crystal Palace instead.

How could a Russian newspaper have had this information only two days after my 'A' sample was opened and before the proper analysis had even started? The results of the BBC's investigation had revealed an incredible train of events that wouldn't have looked out of place in a John Le Carré spy novel.

18 June   I take the dope test in Lisbon.

20 June   The lab receives the test.

7 July   The test is opened. The sample is still only a number.

7–8 July   Alexander Lubinov, a Moscow journalist with *The Sport Express*, is contacted by an 'anonymous source' and told of the positive test.

9 July   The story appears in the Russian newspaper.

18 July   The test results in Lisbon are finally completed.

24 July   The head coach of the Russian Athletics Federation approaches two journalists – Neil Wilson (*Daily Mail*) and Franco Fava (the Italian *Gazzetta della Sport*) – at the Goodwill Games in St Petersburg. The coach repeats the story about a British athlete testing positive. Franco Fava contacts the President of the

Russian Athletics Federation who confirms the story
and reveals (off the record) he knows the name of
the athlete.

Vicente listened to the story that Brendan had uncovered with
increasing alarm. What was going on? How could a Russian
newspaper know about results that had not even been properly
analysed? The press speculated that I was the victim in some
complicated web of conspiracy. We didn't know. The only thing
that was certain was that the test had not been done by the book
and there had been security leaks right from the start. Vicente
felt shocked and disillusioned.

Events that afternoon did nothing to lift his mood. When
Dr Cowan and Professor Beckett finally emerged from the testing
at 4 pm they both looked angry. They reported that the pH level
of the 'B' sample was 8.85. When I had given the sample the level
had been 5, which is normal.

Vicente asked what could have caused this change. They replied
there were two possibilities. One was that the sample had been
stored at the wrong temperature and therefore had deteriorated
badly. It had a bad odour which lent weight to this theory.
The other explanation was that the sample had been spiked.
Dr Cowan, as a representative of the BAF, didn't want to
speculate on this possibility. Both he and Professor Beckett
had wanted to stop the testing since the sample could have
been ruined by bacteria. Dr Dolle of the IAAF, however, had
insisted they continue, as Dr Barbosa promised them full chain
of custody documents before the day was out.

Two hours later they filed back into the office and announced
that the 'B' test was positive. It confirmed the 42:1 ratio between
testosterone and epitestosterone shown in the first sample. It was
the result we had half expected and half dreaded. The promised
chain of custody papers were then handed over. When Vicente
and the others examined them, they were dated 30 August 1994 –
the day of the 'B' test they had just witnessed! The whole point of
the documents was that they should be contemporaneous. Every
time the sample was moved the documents should have been
signed and dated, from the first time they were stored on 18
June at the San Antonio stadium complex. The test had gone
ahead on the assurance that the chain of custody would be

produced and now the documents were not worth the paper they were written on. Vicente was furious – he felt they had been fooled into continuing with the whole charade. Professor Beckett, one of the most respected figures in world dope testing, was equally unhappy. He later went on record to say, 'I almost did not proceed with analysis of the "B" sample in the absence of the appropriate supporting documents of chain of custody. We only agreed to proceed when assurances were given that these documents would be provided.'

The Portuguese staff then announced the 'B' sample analysis documents would not be ready for a few days. Vicente and the others had a plane to catch and they were leaving without vital documents. He reflected darkly that they'd been led round in circles from the hour they'd arrived. There seemed nothing to be gained by staying longer in Lisbon. The mood was sombre as they started the long journey home. Everyone felt that something was wrong – even the BAF representatives looked unhappy. For the moment, they had a more immediate problem to face – getting past the reporters massed outside.

When he finally got home late that night, Vicente told me about his ordeal at the hands of the press. All day the press corps outside the Lisbon laboratory had been building up. There were TV camera crews from several nations and anything from fifty to seventy journalists, waiting in the hallway and barricading the door. From the moment they appeared, Vicente and the other four were mobbed. Vicente had cameras and microphones pushed against his head and shoulders as he tried to force a way through the insane crush. One cameraman stumbled, dropping his camera against Vicente's shin and bruising it badly. It took three or four minutes for all five of the British party to fight their way through the entrance hall to the minibus waiting outside. Even then the van had to move slowly to cut a path through the reporters who were blocking every window.

Once back in London the farce began afresh. Vicente and Malcolm Brown had decided to catch the shuttle flight to Manchester airport that evening. As they left the international gate they found they were besieged by the media again. They set off at a run through the airport with reporters and camera crews chasing madly alongside. Questions were fired at them: 'What happened in Lisbon?' 'Is this test going to prove Diane is innocent?'

Mum and I celebrating my 25th birthday and my engagement to Vicente.

Marit (Vicente's mum) and I enjoying the sun in our first home in Sale, Cheshire, 1991.

1992 Barcelona Olympic Games (Semi-final).

From inside lane – Ella Kovacs (Romania), Ana Quirot (Cuba), Sigrun Wodars (Germany), Ellan Van Langen (Holland), Lyubov Gurina (Russia), Julie Jenkins (USA), Diane Modahl, Carla Sacramento (Portugal).

Very disappointing race.

The term 'love at first sight' doesn't only happen in romantic novels.

Vicente and I looking forward to tucking into the wedding cake made by mum!

Parents and bride and groom joining in the fun. From left: Lena, Di, Vicente, Marit and Sydney.

Me celebrating my 26th birthday with mum and dad at Fridays restaurant, 1992.

Now this is a story in itself. I just had to bring my wedding dress on the honeymoon in Maui, Hawaii –
Vicente meanwhile had other thoughts. 1992.

Part of my portfolio of pictures during the winter of 1992 whilst with the Manchester Model Agency.

My best major Championship performance to date as well as my most consistent year –
breaking 2 minutes, 7 times for the 800m. Finishing in 4th place in the 1993 World Championships
in Stuttgart, Germany.

Finishing second to the 1992 Olympic Champion (Ellan Van Langen) over 1,000m in the McDonalds
Games in Sheffield 1993. Kelly Holmes also in shot. 1993 was such a great year I was very confident that
1994 would be even better.

Photo: Allsport, Neil Loft

Having a bit of fun! June 1994. Just months before we would experience anything like fun in a long time.

Top. Di at the Commonwealth Games in Canada, attending an Official Function day before the Games started. Little did I know that days later everything I believed in would be in ruins. Posing with English gymnasts. From left: Annika Reeder, Jacqueline Brady, Di, Zita Lusack, Karin Szymko.

Centre. I was looking forward so much to defending my title, I was relaxing and enjoying the sights of Canada.

Bottom. Unable to even think about Christmas, we left our home to try and find peace and understand what had happened to us.

They made it on to the shuttle bus which would take them to the plane. At that moment Vicente was glad he wasn't Michael Jackson. Neither he nor Malcolm Brown had ever been at the centre of an international news story before and they both had to laugh at the absurdity of their predicament. Arriving in Manchester, Malcolm Brown said, 'I'll take the pressure. You run and get a taxi while I hold them off. Get back to Diane without them following you.' In the event it didn't work out: there were so many TV crews and reporters waiting at the airport that the two of them got separated in the crush. Vicente forced his way through to a taxi, refusing to answer any questions. He jumped in, shouting to the driver, 'Drive! Just get away! I need to get away!'

They were a few miles down the M56 to Manchester centre when the driver said, 'By the way, have a look behind you. I think we're being followed.' Out the back window, Vicente could see half a dozen cars keeping close to them. Up to that point the press had been unable to find me; now they were hoping Vicente would lead them right to the front door. Vicente prayed that he had picked the right taxi driver. 'Can you lose them?' he asked.

The reply was confident. 'Oh yes, I'll get rid of them.' The driver went on to say he'd been listening to the story on the radio. 'My wife said only today, "First they build up these athletes then they kill them off." Those officials ought to be strung up for what they're doing to Diane. All the neighbours down our way know Diane is innocent. Don't worry, I'll get rid of this lot for you.'

What followed was like a car chase in a Hollywood movie, except that it was played out on the roads to Didsbury and Stockport. The taxi would suddenly make a brake turn in the middle of the road and head back in the opposite direction. A squeal of tyres told that the press pack were turning to follow. The taxi turned down side roads and took corners at Formula One speed, with Vicente bounced around in the back. Some of the pursuers had been lost but a few were still on their tail. The taxi finally gained some ground. It swung sharply into an industrial estate and down a small lane. The driver parked behind some containers and switched off the lights. Suddenly all was quiet. They sat there in the darkness for about ten minutes to make sure they were safe. At one point the silence was disturbed by Vicente's mobile phone.

'Yes?'

'It's Brendan from the BBC. Do you have time to talk?'

Vicente closed his eyes. 'I've seen enough of journalists for one day, thanks. No, I don't want to talk now.'

Vicente was dropped off at Manchester City Football Ground and walked the rest of the way, so as to keep the location of Barbara's house a secret. He handed over a £20 tip. The taxi driver would have a good story to tell his wife when he got home that night.

When he finally reached the door Vicente must have felt his ordeal was finally over. But there was one more trial to face – my twin sisters and I. We'd been waiting up all night for him to arrive and were desperate to hear the full story.

'What happened?' we wanted to know as soon as he was sitting down.

'Oh, so much happened.'

'Yes? Like what?'

'The sample was tested and I didn't understand it all.'

I was getting more and more on edge and he was getting more impatient after the horrendous day he'd endured.

'So what did they suggest? What was the explanation?' I wanted to know.

'There were several explanations,' he answered wearily. 'The sample had deteriorated – maybe that had an effect. Maybe someone tampered with it. Or somebody could have put something in your food, I don't know. It could easily have been a waiter. Dr Cowan told me that all it takes is a little squeeze of something in your food or drink.'

I was desperate for an answer and this sounded like one.

'Really? He said that's possible?'

'Yes, it's possible.'

'Right,' I said. 'I want to know the name of the waiter that day.'

'Oh Diane! I've no idea. I'm just saying it's an example.'

Vicente was getting exasperated but so was I.

'You can't say it's the waiter and then it's not the waiter. You have to have proof! Is it or isn't it?'

My sisters started to join in. There were raised voices and hands waving in the air. This was important. If it was the waiter we wanted his name. 'Give me the name of the waiter!' I was shouting.

Vicente suddenly stood up and exploded. '*Are you all stuffed?* I'm shattered, I'm hungry. I've come home. I've been going through tests all day. I don't know the name of the damn waiter. It was just *an example!*'

For a few seconds there was a heavy silence in the room. Then all four of us burst out laughing. We realised just how stupid it all was. In our eagerness to find an answer we'd started to chase ghosts and lost our grip on reality. Vicente had come home from Lisbon and we were expecting him to give us some solution, some explanation that would clear up the whole mess. The tension of the long exhausting day was released in our laughter. After that evening, the incident became a favourite family joke. For the next two or three months, whenever Vicente entered a room, someone from my family would innocently ask, 'Have you got the name of that waiter yet?' Equally any argument would dissolve in laughter if one of us erupted with Vicente's unique expression, '*Are you all stuffed?*'

It was one of the rare light moments in a bleak and harrowing day. I couldn't avoid the fact that the 'B' sample had confirmed the 'A' test and that we still had no clear answer to what had really happened. It was hard to sleep again that night. It was a setback, but we hadn't given up the fight. Some day soon, I was certain, an explanation would come to light and everyone would realise that the whole episode had been a terrible, tragic mistake.

Chapter 10

On The Rack

They say a lie goes around the world before Truth has time to put its boots on. The lie that I had used performance enhancing steroids was international news before I'd even set foot back in the country. Truth took a bit longer to catch up. A few days later – around the time the 'B' sample was opened in Lisbon – the tide started to turn. The British press started to ask the same questions to which we wanted answers: why was it so long (over nine weeks) before any announcement? Was the Lisbon lab reliable? How could the level of testosterone in my test be so high (the highest ever found in a woman and a staggering four times as high as Ben Johnson's)? It had all started to look suspicious. There was more to 'the Modahl case' than everyone had first assumed.

The change in the way my case was reported was doubly welcome as it meant we could go back to our own home. The initial eruption of media interest had died down. We still saw reporters outside the house but not the mob that had filled our street in the first few days. Some of the press had left beer cans and pizza boxes on garden walls. I could only guess what our neighbours had made of it all. Lesley sent a note round at my request apologising to people for the disruption of their peace.

As we drove up to our own front door, we were both glad to be home. Barbara had been marvellous in taking us in but there is nothing like sleeping in your own bed again. I had been away since 4 August, it was now 2 September and the intervening month felt like a lifetime. Our two Persian cats, Elske and Deilig, took a few cautious sniffs before they remembered me. It was good to be back, yet at the same time I couldn't avoid feeling a sense of anti-climax. All around me were reminders of athletics. My medals were on the wall, my spikes and trainers in the hallway, Vicente's office was littered with signs of his job as a coach and manager – even in our own house there was no escape from the shadow hanging over us.

We read through the mail. All week letters of support had been pouring in. They came from all over Britain and from as far afield as the Falkland Islands. Some were only addressed 'Diane Modahl – England'. People were offering their own experience of irregularities on tests they'd been through for cancer; others just wanted to encourage us to fight on. There were several that moved us to tears. Yet what struck me most was that people had actually sat down to write a letter, bought a stamp and posted it to someone they didn't even know. Those messages helped to carry us through the early days. They also showed us that public opinion was on our side. In all the hundreds of letters we received, only two contained ugly comments, and in both cases the writers lacked the courage to sign their names.

On the first day of September we received another huge boost to our morale: the British women's team would not, after all, be withdrawn from the World Cup. The news arrived by fax at exactly 12.20 pm. We had been watching Ceefax impatiently all morning. During the past days we'd been urging Peter Radford, Chairman of the BAF, to uphold the important principle of presumption of innocence. We understood he was in a very difficult position, under tremendous pressure from the IAAF. Their spokesman, Christopher Winner, actually had the nerve to say, 'Diane Modahl is being selfish over this. It is Britain's moral obligation to pull the team out.'

Peter Radford could only promise us that a meeting was being held and the decision would not be taken lightly. As we saw it, if the British Athletics Federation pulled out, they judged me guilty; if they stayed in, they were upholding the principle of presumption of innocence. When the official fax arrived Lesley phoned us to break the news and we both cried with relief. So much had gone against us that we'd hardly dared hope for the decision to go our way. By taking part in the World Cup the BAF said to the world, we don't believe Diane Modahl is guilty until it is proved. Peter Radford stated: 'To have withdrawn the team at this time could be seen as an assumption of guilt of an individual athlete before it was proven, which could well have the effect of prejudicing that athlete's case and her right to a fair hearing.'

It was a high point and the only support I'd received from the BAF. Yet even on that day, there was little time to celebrate. Later that afternoon we were driving to London for more medical tests, this time to reveal whether I had cancerous cells in my ovaries. Dr Mark Harris (the doctor we'd first met at Northwick Park Hospital on my return from Canada) and Professor Harry Gordon had suggested that my positive testosterone result was exactly equal to that found in women with tumours in their ovaries. Another theory. It was frightening and humiliating the way my body was being discussed by strangers.

Next morning I was back at Northwick Park Hospital undergoing an uncomfortable series of tests. At one point I remember lying on a bed, while two male doctors, a nurse and Vicente all looked intently at a screen to see what was going on inside my body. They were examining my ovaries and discussing me while I lay there. The doctor would say to the nurse, 'Probe a little further to the left' or 'Can you find it more to the right?' Then somebody might turn to me and say, 'Sorry about this, I'm sure it must be awful for you.' It was as if I was hardly a person any more, just a body on a stretcher. Yet I was prepared to endure all the discomfort and embarrassment if it could only reveal the answer.

Afterwards Vicente and I sat in the doctor's office, waiting to hear if I had cancer. There was also a question mark over whether we would be able to have children in the future. It was frightening and unreal. Yet we were just praying for an answer. If I had cancer then we would deal with that later. It would be grave news but we could at least deal with the truth. How can you deal with the lie that you'd taken drugs? You can only deny it so many times. All we wanted to know was if this test could provide an answer to the torment we were enduring.

I wrote in my diary that day: 'People think because you look no different on the outside, that you feel the same inside. How very very wrong. Emotionally I'm being torn apart, I feel utterly alone.'

When the results came there were no definite answers. We were told there would have to be more tests.

*　　*　　*

Back home in Sale, we forced ourselves to go out for a training run. But the emotional strain of the week had been too much for me. Every day we were talking about the case and on this occasion, I couldn't take any more. Vicente said I should try to stay positive. I replied that I couldn't see anything positive. I felt slapped in the face. The sport I'd been involved in since the age of 11 had let me down. We had given up running by this point. I could hardly lift my feet. I stood there in public and began to cry uncontrollably. The tears were streaming down my face and wouldn't stop. I felt that the whole world was staring at me. What was the point in training? There was no destination, there was no desire in me. I couldn't see a future any more.

The training sessions continued five or six times a week over the next months. There were many times like the first when I would stop and ask what was the point of it all. Vicente, as my coach and manager, would urge me to keep going. There was a point in keeping fit, he argued, a point because I was innocent, a point because I might want to come back to athletics some day.

It was hard but we kept training, partly as a way of trying to re-establish a routine. In September I went back to college in Warrington to begin the second year of the media course I'd started in 1993. Friends and family had asked anxiously if I was going back but there was never a question in my mind. At that stage I was still in fast forward mode, determined and defiant that my life would go on as if everything was normal. University provided a welcome escape from the phone and the office, from the need to fight the case which was dominating every hour of our lives. At college I was just another student. People didn't ask me what was happening because I gave a pretty strong impression that I didn't want to discuss it. I looked forward to going to college, and returning home again to the case was hard.

Vicente was the one on the frontline, talking on the phone, writing letters and looking at every possible angle. Reporters were still phoning us every day and their insistent questions put him in a very difficult position. He didn't want to say anything about the case because the hearing was still to come and we didn't want to prejudice my chances. At the same time, if the story was going to be in the papers we wanted it to be reported truthfully; he couldn't just keep saying 'no comment'. In the end, we decided Vicente would only speak about the way we were coping as a couple. Anything the media dug up as evidence came entirely from them.

One of the questions reporters always asked was, 'How is Diane?' and on countless occasions I heard Vicente say, 'She's fine, under the circumstances.' When the phone was down, a familiar argument would begin.

'Vicente, I am not fine. You cannot answer for me. How do you know I'm fine?'

'Well, what else do you expect me to say?'

'You can tell them I'm not fine. I'm feeling awful. I want to scream. Tell them that. Don't give this nice rosy picture that we're fine, "under the circumstances"!'

We had agreed that he would be the one in the frontline, but it created inevitable tensions. He was making decisions and they were about me; even though I usually agreed with the decision, I wanted to make it for myself. I was worried that people would start to see me as a little mouse sitting at home, incapable of even stringing two words together. Maybe they thought it was all going over my head and I had to have a strong husband to speak for me. Anyone who knew me, knew that was far from the truth.

People may ask, why didn't you get on the phone or go on TV and speak for yourself? There were times I wanted to and days when the frustration was almost unbearable, yet 90 per cent of the time I knew we were handling it the best way for both of us. There was never a time when we sat down and planned out our different roles. What had happened from the start was that the phone was ringing and somebody needed to answer it. I was in no fit state to talk to anyone and Vicente was the manager, so he took on the position of spokesman. For one thing I knew that I couldn't do as good a job as Vicente. He was pushing and digging for answers all the time, speaking to lawyers, athletes and medical experts. Obviously as a manager he'd been involved in the administrative side for years. He knew what went on behind the sport while I only knew what happened on the track. There was another reason, which was probably a survival instinct. In all honesty, there was part of me that wanted to block the whole thing out and leave it to someone else.

Where I needed to distance myself, fighting the case was something Vicente needed to retain his sanity. As my coach and husband his business was badly hit by the accusations I was facing.

For weeks the phone had stopped ringing for his athletes and the fax had gone dead. All the phone calls were about me, so he had to feel he was doing something. He has always been someone who deals with a situation by taking action. If a fire breaks out Vicente is the first to jump into the flames and start putting them out. He's not afraid of anyone or anything, which is his great strength. I'm maybe the more calm and patient one, so we had to learn how to make our differences work for us. When Vicente was speaking to Tony or someone else on the phone I would usually hook off the other phone and listen in. Then I would write questions on a note and Vicente would ask them on my behalf. To the world it may have seemed that my husband was the one fighting the case, but really we battled side by side all along the line.

In any case, we soon realised that Vicente was on trial as much as me. We began to hear rumours from other athletes and coaches that my husband was the one who had administered drugs to me. I was 'a nice girl who'd been part of the British team for years', but Vicente was portrayed as this ambitious foreigner who could have been doping me without my knowledge. On 13 September the rumours came out in public with a vicious article in *Today* newspaper. I made a point of not reading the press but Vicente was so angry that he read this article out loud to me. There were no open allegations or evidence against him, just a thin tissue of lies and insinuations meant to create the impression that there was something untrustworthy about my husband.

According to the article Vicente was 'a mysterious figure even to those closest to him'. 'Outwardly he is a respectful, gentle man. But little is known of his past even among the athletes who are contracted to his Manchester based company "Modahl International".' The same reporter went on to 'reveal' that Norwegian sprinter Aham Okeke, one of my so-called 'training partners', had been banned for a positive drug test. The implication was obvious to anyone who read the article: Vicente was the sinister influence behind both cases.

There were a few facts the article conveniently left out. Vicente's only official connection with Okeke was that they belonged to the same athletics club in Norway. He had acted unofficially as an agent to get Okeke races but the athlete wasn't contracted to him and he certainly wasn't Okeke's coach. Vicente had never had anything to do with his training, what he ate or anything else. As for me, I had never trained with Aham Okeke in my life. I can think of only one occasion where we were on the same track and he was on the other side, working with his own coach. He is a 100 metres runner, I run 800 metres; he lives in Norway, I live in Manchester. To call him my training partner was beyond belief.

As for Vicente being a 'mystery man', we wondered why the great investigative reporter, Nigel Whitefield, had never bothered to phone and ask Vicente directly about his childhood and background. The article didn't bother to ask why Vicente would have doped his own wife without her knowledge. He had little to gain and everything to lose by it. He would have risked not only my reputation but his own and his whole career as a coach, agent and manager for a number of world-class athletes.

Of course certain journalists are only interested in a story that sells newspapers, but we had to suffer the impact on our lives and our livelihood. The story started a rumour campaign about Vicente. International athletics is a competitive world and there were plenty of people who'd have enjoyed seeing Vicente's reputation ruined and his athletes going elsewhere. Soon after the article, a sponsor for a prestigious high jump meet that Vicente was organising in Liverpool pulled out. A number of sponsors started to make excuses where before they had been keen to work with him. The story was the same in Portugal where Brendan Pittaway confirmed several coaches wanted Vicente out.

We began to wonder how much worse things could get. People were taking advantage of the difficult situation we were in with rumours and accusations that had no basis in the truth. Watching my husband suffer, I felt sad and disillusioned once more. We were two honest, positive and basically optimistic people; we weren't bad – why was this happening to us? It may be difficult for anyone to understand the scale of pressure we faced on every side. One day I would be undergoing medical tests to reveal whether I had cancer, the next we might be asking whether we'd have to sell our house to pay for the costs of the case. My family were suffering badly and ringing for news all the time, while the two of us stood in the middle, trying desperately to hold our lives together whilst pouring all our energy into the fight to clear my name.

The financial implications hit us the first month after the Commonwealth Games. Literally overnight we lost all my income.

Anything that I'd earned from athletics backdated to June was immediately withheld. As a favourite in the Commonwealth Games, a member of the British World Cup team, and with a three-year sponsorship deal with Nike, I'd just reached the stage where I was beginning to make a comfortable income from athletics. All that was wiped out at one go on 24 August. My income was literally zero and I was unable to take part in any meetings until my name was cleared.

On top of this, Vicente's business was cut by half. Five of his athletes left in the months following Victoria and several sponsorship deals fell through. All this we could have weathered – money was the last thing we were thinking about – except that we were fighting a case against the IAAF, and the cost was crippling us. In early September we had to make our first payment for our legal and experts' costs. It was dawning on us just how much fighting the case was going to cost. We had already lost over half of our income and we now had to find thousands of pounds to pay our legal bills. The question of where we were going to find the money was one that worried us both. Vicente thought we would have to consider selling the house.

Christopher Winner, IAAF's spokesman, stated in an interview that week, 'If Diane Modahl was Romanian, she would have been found guilty by now. Just because she lives in a Western country like Britain and she has heavyweight lawyers and medical experts, she is still able to prepare her case.' We did have the best lawyers and experts we could find, but we were two people up against the whole powerful, unfair system. Were we supposed to lie down and die when I was innocent? Did Mr Winner know anything about the emotional and financial cost to us? We stood to lose our savings, our house, everything we owned, including what was most precious of all: our reputations. It was in the hardest times that we learnt who our true friends were. David Grindley, the British 400 metres champion, who is one of Vicente's athletes, told us that if we had to leave our own house he would buy us a terraced house to live in. It was an offer that we could never accept but one that meant more than we could say.

On the same day that we received our first legal bill, I talked to my mother again for the first time since my return. It was beautiful to hear her voice, even though she sounded tired and depressed. Her own mother had died recently and, with my ordeal, she felt like she'd been through two funerals in the past month. My father was also suffering badly. When the news broke he was alone in the house. Somebody had phoned to tell him to switch on his television set. The next thing he knew was that there were reporters hammering on his door. I hadn't had any chance to warn my family I was being sent home. The shock particularly affected my father, who'd always been proud of his youngest daughter's achievements. He was the one who polished my medals and kept my scrapbook in order. The neighbours all knew my name and he would proudly tell his work mates if I was running in the European Championships, Commonwealth Games or a Grand Prix meeting. Suddenly, that day in August, he found himself staring at the television screen and hearing his own daughter publicly accused of cheating. It was painfully hard for him to cope with; whenever I visited he would cry and hug me. I could see that he felt totally helpless.

I would try to avoid talking about the case when I was at my parents' house. It became almost like a swear word in the house. We did our best to go back to the old Sunday dinners with the family around the table. Dad's music was playing in the background and we were all eating, drinking and making jokes. Then inevitably, towards the end of the meal, someone would ask, 'How is the case going?' and the atmosphere would change; we were back into the endless circle of what was happening and what we should do. I knew that my family were suffering too. They were doing everything they could to help and support us, but in the end I just needed them to be my family. I couldn't cope with their suffering and bewilderment on top of my own. There had to be some escape from this heavy burden which we carried round with us everywhere.

In the end it was Vicente that brought the matter to a head, although I didn't thank him for it at the time. Paula was at our house one day and I heard Vicente tell her, 'I've had a word with Diane's family and I told them that they're not allowed to talk about the case.' Paula agreed that it was the right thing, but it was news to me and I was furious. When Paula went, I confronted Vicente. 'How dare you tell my family not to talk about the case?'

'Diane, I'm doing it for you,' he protested. 'When you go round there you don't want to hear about the case. You want to hear about the family, your sisters and brothers. You don't need the strain of answering questions about what's going on and what the lawyer is doing.'

'But that's okay. I want the opportunity to tell them more. It's not up to you to decide who can say what and who can't.'

Vicente could see how upset and angry I was, he admitted it was a mistake and apologised. But a week later it was my turn to admit I'd been wrong. I couldn't carry the burden of supporting my family as well. Of course I knew they weren't asking me for support but I was bound to feel I was partly responsible for relieving their pain. Sometimes I would hear myself on the phone saying, 'Oh, don't worry, it's not that bad,' when I knew it was worse than bad, it was unbearable. The next Sunday I had a heart to heart with my mother and told her what I'd decided. We would have to avoid dragging up the case when I was with my family. I wasn't able to take on their emotions and need for support as well. I was so much in need of support myself that I had nothing left to give.

We were still waiting to hear a date for the BAF hearing. Until then we were in limbo. The case seemed to drag on, days became weeks and weeks, months and 24 August was slipping further and further into the past. Some days we were on a high as some new evidence came to light, other days we felt terribly low when nothing seemed to be happening. There were documents that still hadn't been sent from Portugal – the chain of custody papers still hadn't arrived by the beginning of October. Our request to have the sample independently tested in London had also been rejected by the IAAF. What did they have to hide?

Tony suggested that the hearing might be postponed until the New Year, if important documents didn't arrive. The idea of the case dragging on that long was unthinkable. Both of us wanted to avoid further delays. Every morning we woke up and the familiar anxieties would crowd in on us again. Was I seriously ill? Why had the Portuguese authorities and the Lisbon lab made so many mistakes? Had anyone spiked my food or drink or tampered with the sample? We needed answers and a final verdict, but it had to be the right one.

During October we were back in London for more medical tests and to hear results from previous tests. We were told by phone that I did have a medical condition – but we would have to wait for more details. We sat in a waiting room for hours while four learned doctors went through my results. The waiting was painful. What was wrong with me and did it provide an answer to the positive test? This time would there be proof?

Professor Harry Gordon beckoned us in. He explained that I had a very rare medical condition that only occurs in South and Central America and the Caribbean. It was a defect in the chromosomes that I'd inherited from one of my parents. It would only affect us having children if Vicente also had the defect, so he had to be tested as well. (The tests later proved negative.)

Our experts confirmed that this medical condition *could* have been the cause of my positive test. The condition prevented my natural testosterone from changing into dihydrotestosterone. For a moment our hopes soared, only to be dashed again as Professor Gordon went on. There was no research into this condition so it couldn't be confirmed as conclusive proof. The connection could be shown which cast doubt on the Lisbon test, but without research, it was not a proven explanation.

Where did it all leave us? Had we just made a giant step forward? Again it felt as if a door had been opened a crack only to be slammed in my face again. Back in the hotel that night I ran away. Vicente was on the phone to Lesley. She asked 'How is Di coping?' and he answered, 'Not bad.' It was too much to take and I ran away to the top of the hotel. I sat on the stairs with my head in my hands and cried. The cleaning supervisor found me and wanted to know if I was okay. I told him I just needed to be alone. I was not okay or coping or 'not bad', I was sick at heart and hated my life. For the whole of the past week I'd been suffering from severe headaches.

Just over a week later we were back in London, this time to see Professor Howard Jacobs in Harley Street. I'm told every national newspaper had been calling Harley Street to try and find the experts handling my case but since I was registered as Miss Diane Max, they'd all drawn a blank. Professor Jacobs was working alongside Dr John Honour at the University College London Medical School. They were both recognised as experts in their field and our hopes were pinned on them. Professor Jacobs had a surprise in store for us: a second medical condition had been found. It seemed I had something called polycystic ovaries, which meant there were a number of cysts on my ovaries. (It is a fairly common problem in women who use the contraceptive pill.) There was no question of cancer and we would be able to have a family. As to the Lisbon result, it could have had a bearing. In severe cases the condition might produce more testosterone and I had been taking the pill for four years before Lisbon, but again the connection could not be proved. There was too little research on testosterone in women.

I felt frustrated and let down yet again. Another medical condition had been found but why didn't it provide an answer that could be proved? Vicente asked if it was possible that the deteriorated urine sample could have produced the unusual peak in testosterone. Professor Jacobs said that this was an interesting point and suggested that Dr Honour store one of my samples in bad conditions to see the effect. Vicente had been trying to make this point for two months and felt at last that someone was listening. Who could say what changes took place in a sample full of bacteria?

We went out for a meal in our favourite Mexican restaurant later. Afterwards we almost fell asleep watching a film. It helped us to forget for a while. The hearing was drawing nearer but the future seemed bleak to me. The strain of fighting the case was starting to tell on me mentally and physically. My headaches had persisted for three weeks and it was an effort even to go for a walk. We were not just fighting the case, we were fighting to survive within ourselves.

At the end of October we had an unexpected visitor: Susan Deaves, the England team manager, whose unhappy job it had been to send me home from Canada. She was very concerned to find out how I was and wanted to talk through the events of that terrible day, 24 August. The whole experience had obviously had a disturbing impact on her; she was the one who'd been forced to break the news and at one point, she truly believed the shock might have been fatal to me. With hindsight, she told us she was sad that I was sent home on the same plane as Paul Edwards. Vicente and I have great respect for her and feel that she did everything that was within her power at the time.

There was also encouragement of a different kind from Brendan Pittaway, the reporter carrying out his own investigation of my case with the BBC. He'd just returned from a trip to Portugal where he'd interviewed many important figures involved in the case. He sent us a copy of the interview transcripts. We knew Brendan's investigation into my case was nearing completion and we awaited the results, to be broadcast on BBC radio and television, with some anxiety.

The hearing was now only weeks away and our case was beginning to look stronger. Ever since Victoria, we'd been looking for one simple answer that would explain the mystery of how I could have tested positive in Lisbon when I had never taken steroids in my life. Scientifically proving something that happened six months ago was not an easy task. It was impossible to reproduce the original sample in the same conditions that had led to the allegations, especially since we believed the samples had been ruined by bacteria. This was one of the key arguments for the hearing. What was more, we could show that the case against me was riddled with holes. The onus of proof was not on us; the BAF had to prove beyond reasonable doubt that administration of testosterone *actually took place*. As our barrister said, their case was so weak it would not have lasted two minutes in a court of law.

What was the case for my innocence? Hundreds of newspaper columns and hours of air time had been devoted to it, but the arguments were so wrapped in scientific jargon that it was often hard for ordinary members of the public to know what was the truth.

Newspapers claimed that we put forward a medical condition as the main defence at my hearing. In fact that wasn't the case. The link with a medical condition couldn't be proved from existing research so we didn't concentrate on that possibility. In any case, we had stronger evidence. The files used in the hearing were several inches thick and would make heavy reading, but the main arguments in my defence are summarised below. Taken together, they show that there were so many real doubts and questions about the case against me that it was almost incredible that it went ahead. The reason we believe it did was that once the IAAF had condemned me, they couldn't afford to be proved wrong. Christopher Winner made that plain well before the hearing even took place, when he said, 'As far as we are concerned she is guilty.'

Reasons why the case against me should not have been brought

1. There was no proof *that the sample was mine, or that it hadn't been spiked*

It is of fundamental importance in any system of sample testing, where important consequences will follow from the result of the test, that a laboratory should be able to show, beyond doubt, that the sample given was the sample tested. This applies to doping control, but also applies to all laboratory systems, as it is part of basic good laboratory practice.

It is not for the athlete to prove that the sample was spiked or tampered with in any way. The integrity of the system is guaranteed by the knowledge that an accredited laboratory of the IOC can *prove* that the sample given was the sample tested. The onus is on the laboratory to show this. The system can only work if all athletes and the public at large can be completely confident in the finding of laboratories. If the laboratory cannot prove beyond a shadow of a doubt that they are testing the correct, unadulterated sample, then the sample should not be tested. The implications of a positive result for an athlete who is innocent are almost unthinkable. It is worse than being accused of a criminal offence. The public vilification which followed my being sent home from Victoria was far worse than most criminals endure. I was branded a cheat, and when I protested my innocence, I was branded a liar.

The IAAF's own rules, set out in the International Olympic Committee's Guidelines, specify that a chain of custody must exist, which shows the progress of the sample from the time it is given until the time it is tested. These documents provide the evidence required to maintain the athletes' and the public's confidence. It would be perfectly easy for the IAAF to have no rules relating to the chain of custody, but they do have these strict rules, because they recognise the importance of faith being maintained in their system.

It is interesting to note that the Guidelines have a 'catch all' phrase which says that an athlete may still be found guilty of a doping offence if the breaches of IOC Guidelines do not amount to *material* breaches. Indeed, in a paper given by Mark Gay, the IAAF lawyer, in Monte Carlo in January 1991 he stated that:

'Arguments based on the chain of custody have a superficial attraction . . . use of the Envopak system provides almost fool proof evidence that the sample taken was indeed that of the athlete.'

Unfortunately this is not true. It is well documented from sources such as the transcript of the Harry 'Butch' Reynolds hearing in the USA and a video made by Sky Television, that the Envopak system is not tamper proof. The pack can be opened in a matter of seconds, and re-sealed just as easily, leaving no evidence of interference.

The IOC Guidelines also specify that this chain of custody must be made contemporaneously, that is, at the time the sample is actually being transported. So when the sample has been given, and sealed in the presence of the athlete, the person who seals it must initiate a chain of custody by signing for it, and stating the time they received it. When it is handed to somebody else, for example a courier, they too must sign for it and again state the time that they received it. If the courier then hands it to the laboratory reception, they also must sign for it and state the time they received it, and so it goes on. All these signatures and timings will be on the same piece of paper attached to the sample, or batch of samples.

To the uninitiated, this may appear to be extremely complex and not something likely to be practised routinely by anybody. In fact the Doping Control Unit of the Sports Council of the United Kingdom, run by Michele Verroken, does this routinely, as do many other worldwide doping control organisations. It is regarded as a vital part of their work and high standards are maintained.

What was the chain of custody for my sample?

The chain of custody in my case consisted of a two page summary written by the laboratory director *after* the 'B' test had been done, and signed but undated written statements only produced the evening before the disciplinary hearing in December.

The two page summary could just as easily have been written by me. It contained no information which I could not have found out after a few minutes of research. The signed but undated written statements were general statements of what the persons concerned would normally expect to happen to samples in their custody. With the exception of one or two people, who claimed to remember the specific batch of samples which my sample was in (heaven knows how they remembered one specific batch in statements they gave five months later), all those who had handled the sample gave vague statements to the effect that they must have done X Y or Z with the sample because that is what they normally do.

Dr Cowan, the head of the only IOC accredited laboratory in the United Kingdom, gave evidence on behalf of the BAF that he did not consider the chain of custody to be adequate.

He is also on record as saying, in a Sky TV programme shown on 8 July, that: 'If we find that the chain of custody has been breached so badly, then we would say there is no purpose in carrying out the analysis, and we would decline to do the analysis.'

Professor Manfred Donike, who is in charge of worldwide IOC accreditation of laboratories in an article entitled 'Laboratory Procedures', published in *Doping is Cheating: Fight for a Clean Sport* at the IAAF 1st World Anti-Doping Seminar, 14–16 March, states:

> There is a well known proverb in analytical chemistry that says errors made at the sample taking stage will determine the analytical result. In doping control, simple, reasonable measures have been laid down in the Procedural Guidelines to guarantee correct sample taking and to maintain the integrity of the sample.

> The 'Chain of Custody' which begins with the urine voiding and ends with the analysis result report, must be impeccable before a positive finding can lead to sanctions.

2. The sample was so degraded it should never have been tested
When the 'B' test was done in front of the observers from the BAF and from my team, it became quite clear at the start that

the sample had deteriorated dramatically. When the sample was given in June its pH value was tested and found to be pH 5. At the time the sample was opened for testing at the end of August, the pH value was measured in two different ways, and one showed a pH of 8.8, the other a pH of 8.9. Thus the pH value was taken to be pH 8.85.

The sample also gave off a strong smell of ammonia. This could mean only one thing – bacteria had been growing in the sample and had changed it. Samples deteriorated to a level above pH 7.5 are generally not tested because any results found may not be accurate. Samples allowed to deteriorate to above pH 7.5 are normally thrown away, and Dr Cowan, in his evidence at the hearing on behalf of the BAF, stated that he himself would not have tested the sample.

The pH value is a measure of the alkalinity of the sample. It is a logarithmic measure. This means that when the pH value goes from 5 to 6 the increase in bacterial contamination of the sample is approximately 10 fold. The same applies to each further value increase, so that if a sample goes from pH 5 to almost pH 9 (as in my case) the bacterial contamination will have increased 10,000 times.

Dr Malcolm Brown specifically pointed this out to the disciplinary panel in December, and all the experts who appeared on my behalf argued that it was ludicrous to use such a degraded sample to test for any banned drug, and testosterone in particular. This is because the bacteria which are known to be present in the urine of any individual are capable, under the right circumstances, of transforming the natural steroids in the urine into other steroids. Of course, this does not normally ever come up because no other laboratories, or IOC accredited laboratories, ever test such degraded samples. IOC Guidelines state that samples with a pH of 7.5 should not normally be tested.

The chain of custody said that the 'B' sample was frozen as soon as it arrived at the laboratory. If this was true, then the degradation must have occurred before the 'A' and 'B' samples arrived at the laboratory. This means the 'A' sample would have been as degraded as the 'B' sample when it was tested – although in a striking example of laboratory incompetence no pH test for alkalinity was done on the 'A' sample by the Portuguese laboratory.

How the samples came to be so degraded is another matter. According to the chain of custody, after the sample was given, the 'A' and 'B' bottles were stored in a locked room for 40 hours before they were taken by a courier to the laboratory. The courier took approximately 1 hour to get from the room to the laboratory. The chain of custody does not state whether the samples were refrigerated for the time they were left in this room. I can only presume, as did my legal team, that the samples were unrefrigerated. This belief was confirmed by the BAF, who produced at the hearing weather details from *The Times* for the temperature in Lisbon on the relevant days (approx 75°F).

The BAF also raised the point that there were 8 samples in total kept under the same conditions, three of which were samples from female athletes. Yet it is very well documented that because of the almost infinite number of variables which go towards the make-up of any one urine sample, different urine samples will change their pH value at different rates. Some hardly change their pH value at all over some days, others like mine change their pH value very rapidly (as has been shown in subsequent tests done on me). It could be that other samples from the same batch deteriorated to the same extent, and did not form testosterone. This is because there are so many different factors which cause the make-up of urine such as diet, skin cells, the amount of sweat which falls into the sample, stress, the level of physical exercise, the sex of the athlete, intestinal bacteria (especially in females), and a multitude of other factors. To achieve the right steroidal reactions to form testosterone is to some extent a matter of chance. All the ingredients for its formation are present in the urine 'soup', and, dependent upon all of the factors listed above and more, testosterone may be formed.

There is, of course, very little experimental work which has been done on standing urine samples, because nobody ever normally leaves them unrefrigerated or unfrozen, and there is no scientific interest in this area. Why should there be? There is, however, a vast body of evidence in the main scientific journals which shows that all of the reaction steps required to form testosterone via a number of different routes have been shown to be possible under conditions similar or the same as those of a degraded urine sample.

3. The laboratory staff were not competent

When the 'A' test was performed no pH test was ever done. This is contrary to standard laboratory practice. Even A level chemistry students would not undertake any form of analysis of something such as a urine sample without first doing a pH test. At the 'B' test, no pH test was going to be done by the Portuguese until Dr Cowan mentioned it. If observers had not been present at the 'B' test, likely as not, the level of degradation would never have been known.

At the hearing it came out that Dr Cowan had had to prevent a member of the laboratory staff from opening a bottle of neat testosterone on the same laboratory bench as the open sample. This again is contrary to standard laboratory practice. If you are looking for a trace substance appearing in minutely small quantities, you do not open a bottle of the neat powder of that substance on the same laboratory bench. One grain of the neat powder would be enough to distort the result completely.

Dr Cowan in his evidence before the disciplinary committee admitted that nothing he saw at the Lisbon laboratory persuaded him the staff were competent. This verdict came from one of the BAF's own experts.

4. The 'B' test should not have gone ahead

Dr Barbosa, who conducted the 'A' and 'B' tests, assured Dr Cowan and Professor Arnold Beckett that the chain of custody documents were all in order. This was in response to their concern that they had not been shown any chain of custody before the 'B' sample took place. After receiving these assurances Dr Cowan and Professor Beckett reluctantly allowed the 'B' test to go ahead on the strength of the promise made by Dr Barbosa. In Dr Cowan's witness statement enclosed in the hearing documents, he said:

> 'Although no chain of custody documents were available, we were assured that they were all in order'

At the hearing itself Dr Cowan said that when he was assured the documents existed he believed what he was being told, and that he found it unacceptable that the documents were not produced after the 'B' test, and still have not been produced.

A 'B' test should only be permitted to go ahead, according to the IOC Guidelines, if the chain of custody documents are in order. They were not, and the test should never have proceeded.

5. *The laboratory data did not confirm the presence of testosterone*

There are two different methods which may be used when scanning a urine sample (using gas chromatography – mass spectrometry (GC-MS)) for anabolic steroids. One is called selected ion monitoring and the other is full scan analysis.

In Lisbon, the primary determination of the ratio of testosterone/epitestosterone concentrations was based on the first procedure, selected ion monitoring. During the 'B' series of analyses full scanning was employed once only. In a full scan, testosterone would be indicated by the presence of four main ions. Of these ions, only one – the 432 ion – was present on the Lisbon full scan. Scientists at the U.S. Food and Drug Administration, for example, consider the identification of a compound by GC-MS/selected ion monitoring to be confirmed only when the analysis includes the detection of *three* characteristic ions. Thus, the U.S. Food and Drug Administration would, if they were to view the data, not regard the evidence from the Lisbon laboratory to confirm the presence of testosterone.

For anybody with a scientific background I have, for completeness, enclosed a table below of what should have been done at the 'A' test under the recommended IOC Guidelines procedure:

1. Verify pH of urine	Not done
2. Verify the colour and appearance. Is the urine dilute?	Not done
3. Perform screening test for anabolic steroids	7th July 1994
4. Screen for natural steroid metabolites and T/E ratio	14th July 1994
5. Perform additional tests with residue of first extract	Not done
6. Re-extract urine	Identical procedure to first test
7. Modify extraction	

(remove free steroids then
glucuronidase hydrolysis)   Not done
  8. Modify derivative   Not done
  9. Full mass spectrum   Not done
10. Specific selected ion
monitoring with adequate
criteria for identification
(e.g. 432, 417, 342, 301)   Not done
11. Verify all information
collected in agreement with
known facts   Not reported

Analysis of the 'B' sample (IOC procedural Guidelines):

2 or 3 aliquots of the 'B' sample	2 aliquots taken
Aliquot of the 'A' sample	None available
A reagent blank e.g. tap water	This was performed
A blank urine, if it is necessary to demonstrate the biological background	Not done
A reference urine collected after application of dope agent	Not done

It is patently clear even to a non-expert that the IOC procedural Guidelines were not adhered to, with the precision which might be expected of an accredited laboratory. Given the support by Professor Manfred Donike to the Lisbon laboratory on the basis of their findings perhaps this is the level of precision which may well be expected of an IOC accredited laboratory. Professor Donike is in charge of IOC laboratory accreditation. He has never questioned the findings of the laboratory, something which he has done in the past if he has had concerns about a case, such as that of Ulrike Heidelmann, the German athlete, who had her positive T/E finding overturned. Despite his other statements, he has also never publically questioned the chain of custody documentation.

6. The findings were not consistent
with testosterone administration

It is well documented that when testosterone is administered various breakdown products (called metabolites) will be formed.

These products are formed when testosterone is broken down by the liver as part of its normal function of purifying the body. The level of testosterone metabolites will always rise if testosterone has, by whatever means, been absorbed into the body.

The level of testosterone metabolites in the reported findings of the Lisbon laboratory were between *one half and one seventh* of what would be normally expected in any given female, as part of their natural hormonal make-up. If I had taken testosterone, then the level of testosterone metabolites would be expected to be *two to three times higher* than normal. So, in finding that I had taken testosterone, the laboratory were, contrary to the IOC Guidelines, ignoring overwhelming evidence that any testosterone which they *may* have found in my sample was *not* due to administration.

At the disciplinary hearing in December we provided very good evidence that *if* there was any testosterone in my sample it was due to the sort of steroidal transformation referred to above. It could not have been due to administration because of the exceptionally low levels of metabolites, when exceptionally high levels would be expected.

After the December hearing we discovered even stronger evidence that the sort of steroidal conversions we had put forward can easily occur given the right circumstances.

7. The T/E ratio was ambiguous

Aside from all these other concerns about whether or not it was testosterone, was the question of the supposed ratio. A T/E ratio is derived from measuring the testosterone peak and the epitestosterone peak. On the data produced by the Lisbon laboratory, there were two equally valid epitestosterone peaks which could have been used to determine the T/E ratio. The Lisbon laboratory chose the peak giving a much higher ratio (42:1 instead of 8:1). There was no good reason for this. The Lisbon laboratory also recorded as approximately 15:1 the standard testosterone which had been measured out as 10:1 If the same margin of error applied to a finding of an 8:1 recorded T/E ratio, then the actual T/E ratio would be just over 5:1 This ratio would be under the IOC limit, and is in fact a ratio that I have been previously recorded as having, by Dr Cowan's laboratory in an out of competition test.

Summary

These are the principal reasons why the case against me should not have been brought. There were many other areas of concern, including the fact that the laboratory had moved from its proper site to the city morgue whilst renovations were taking place at the laboratory. This begged the question whether the laboratory that performed the tests was actually accredited as meeting IOC standards. When this was raised at the hearing, Dr Cowan argued that accreditation was given to the individual who heads the laboratory as opposed to the physical site of the laboratory itself, and he cited IAAF rules, which although not clear on this point, seemed to allow Dr Cowan's interpretation.

The fact remains, however, that the laboratory had its re-accreditation test in March 1994, and then moved to an altogether different site at the city morgue building. The re-accreditation test covers all aspects of importance, such as security, storage of samples, personnel, and equipment. One can presume that the personnel made the move, but did all the equipment? Did the security? Certainly, nobody who went out to Lisbon to witness the 'B' test was aware of any security at the building housing the city morgue, nor the third floor of that building which was the precise location of the 'new' laboratory. Of course, one may well wonder why the re-accreditation test needs to take place at all, if it is perfectly acceptable for a laboratory to shift across town to a completely different location and set up shop there. Why not just ask the heads of all laboratories to go to Cologne and be re-accredited there by Professor Donike. After all it is they who are accredited, apparently, and not the laboratory. In the letter by Prince Alexandre de Merode of 17 June 1994 to all interested parties, he lists 7 laboratories of the 1994 total of 24, which have been downgraded, thus restricting their activities. He then states:

> . . . we are currently in the process of implementing the necessary corrected procedures and trust that these laboratories will soon be fully operational once again.

How do you implement the necessary corrective procedures to the head of a laboratory?

The policy of the IAAF seems to be that where some ambiguity in the rules comes to light, then Professor Manfred Donike is asked for his opinion. In this case, in a letter of 5 December 1994 produced at the Hearing in December, Professor Donike affirmed Dr Cowan's belief that accreditation was given to a laboratory as an institution and in particular to the Head of the laboratory. he also said that moving location was acceptable, so long as the rules were followed. He also stated:

> At the occasion of the last Cologne Workshop in Dope Analysis in April this year Dr J. Barbosa informed me about the intended reconstruction of the laboratory space and the temporary hospitality granted in the rooms of the Institute of Legal Medicine.

Obviously, if it is the Head of the laboratory who is accredited, then he or she can move the laboratory anywhere, as and when they please. Dr Barbosa was therefore not seeking permission from Professor Donike by telling him this (Professor Reys is Head of the laboratory). For some reason, Professor Donike thought it important enough to mention in a letter.

Another area of concern was that of confidentiality. It is regarded as a very important feature of IOC accredited laboratories, and all other laboratories, that confidentiality is maintained. Amazingly enough a Russian newspaper reported that a British female athlete had tested positive for anabolic steroids, two days after the 'A' test had started. The 'A' test began on 7 July, and this information came out on 9 July in the paper.

The 'A' test was concluded on 18 July. I was not informed of the result of this test until 28 August, over nine weeks later. I have to wonder whether it is more than an unfortunate coincidence when positive drug test results are announced at major competitions. I was given my result only hours before I was due to defend my Commonwealth title, a time which guaranteed maximum publicity for the effectiveness of dope testing procedures. I was then given two days in which to attend the 'B' test, or to let it go ahead without any representation. Given the general standard of the laboratory which emerged at the 'B' test, it is frightening to think that all this information may never have come to light.

Nobody from Portugal was prepared to come over and defend

their findings. The laboratory report was not signed. The original witness statements were not signed. The ones that arrived the evening before the Hearing in December were signed but not dated. Mark Gay, the IAAF lawyer, asked them to come over and give evidence in a letter dated 2 December. Professor Mirandela da Costa said that the witnesses could not come over because they were civil servants, the British press was hostile, and if the BAF wanted, the enquiries could take place in Portugal. This sums up the attitude of those who provided the evidence upon which I was found guilty. Despite all the manifest breaches of procedure and standard laboratory practice, they would not come and defend their findings, because they may be criticised by the Press. I, meanwhile, was accused of being a cheat and a liar. This evidently did not concern them an iota. They did not even respond to the joint requests of the BAF and our experts, for further information.

It should also be noted that Istvan Gyulai of the IAAF stated on 13 July 1995, among a wealth of similar statements from the IAAF, and in particular Christopher Winner, that: 'The IAAF is pretty confident that the job done by the Portuguese laboratory was impeccable.'

The IAAF were given a copy of the transcript of the December Hearing, and so were fully aware of all that happened in Lisbon. To all my fellow athletes, I wish you luck when you give your next urine sample.

These were disturbing questions, which had far-reaching implications not only for my own case but for the whole future of dope testing in international athletics. A week before the hearing was due to take place, Brendan Pittaway revealed the findings of his investigation for the BBC. The effect was instantly explosive.

Note   Professor Manfred Donike died from a heart attack on 21 August 1995, aged 61.

Chapter 11

Judgement Day

On 4 December, nine days before the hearing in London was due to take place, we had a phone call from Brendan Pittaway at the BBC. The story he had been working on for three months was about to break at 1.35 pm that day, on Radio 5 Live's *On the Line* programme. Brendan had wanted to wait until almost immediately before the hearing, but his bosses at the BBC wanted to make sure they had broken an exclusive story before the rest of the media.

We sat down to listen to the twenty-five minute programme nervously. We had no control over what was said. We'd asked them to uncover the truth, even if it was painful or costly for us. The extent of our co-operation was only to supply some names and addresses, otherwise the whole investigation was the work of Brendan and his colleagues at the BBC. What had they found out? Would it be accurate and, crucially, what effect would it have, coming out so close to the hearing? As Brendan's familiar voice came over the radio, we listened on the edge of our seats.

The story had been well researched and was a fair summary of events. There were interviews with most of the people involved in my case, including David Grindley, Sue Deaves, Professor Beckett, Dr David Cowan and Peter Radford of the BAF. Professor Beckett explained how he had nearly stopped the analysis of the 'B' sample and had been misled into continuing. Malcolm Brown talked about the alterations made to my results on the screening document. This showed the analysis results of all the athletes at Lisbon. Next to my name the letter 'N' (presumably No) had been changed in a different pen and handwriting to the letter 'Y'.

Brendan had also managed to interview Dr Barbosa and other staff at the Lisbon lab. From these interviews he concluded: 'Senior sources in Portugal admitted the analysts didn't even consider the possibility of a medical explanation for the highest ever level of testosterone ever found in a female athlete.' According to IOC and IAAF guidelines I should have immediately been told if my test suggested there was any possibility of a medical condition. I heard nothing until over nine weeks later. These facts, together with the full story of the leak to the Russian newspaper, presented a damning picture of mistakes, bad practice and plain deceit.

The response from the rest of the media was immediate. Suddenly all the damaging questions about events in Lisbon were out in the open. It was the leading story on the BBC 1 news that evening and a large part of the programme was devoted to the flaws in the case against me. Rob Bonnett closed the report with the words, 'All this will weigh heavily in her favour at this month's BAF hearing. It would be a major surprise if she was not cleared.'

The phone was ringing constantly. It was like the first weeks after I had been sent home from Canada, only this time the world was on our side and it was the IAAF who were in the dock. As well as speaking to journalists from Belfast to Bristol, we had phone calls of support from Linford Christie, John Regis, David Grindley, Steve Smith, Kevin McKay, Paula Thomas, Tessa Sanderson and many more too numerous to mention. The postman again started to work overtime on our road, delivering letters from doctors, professors, friends, fans and churches. We were being swept along on a tidal wave of support towards the hearing. The newspaper headlines next morning were also dominated by the news. Even *Today*, the one newspaper that had consistently attacked us, ran the headline, 'Diane holds all the cards'. Predictably, the only dissenting voice came from Christopher Winner of the IAAF who didn't like all the bad publicity directed against them. 'It is unfortunate that such a flood of information is coming out before the hearing because it stands to become prejudicial,' complained Winner. 'The fact is that there is a *prima facie* case against Diane Modahl. If this is not proved she will be welcomed back into the world of athletics. But we are not close to that, and, at the moment, this mounting hysteria is putting pressure on the impartiality of the hearing.'

Again we were being accused of orchestrating our own media campaign. In fact we'd had very little to do with the BBC *On the Line* programme. The fact that it went out ten days before the hearing was completely beyond our control. At the same time we were turning down offers of around a quarter of a million pounds to sell our story to the tabloid newspapers. If we wanted publicity or money it was there for the asking, but we wanted something far more important: the truth. If my trial had been judged by the public there was little doubt who would have won. In the three months before the hearing I was stopped all the time by members of the public who just wanted to show their support. An off-duty policeman one day stopped me outside Tesco's. 'You don't remember me, do you?' he said. I admitted I didn't.

'I was the constable who drove the van down to Wembley with you all when your brother Clive was competing in the ABA (Amateur Boxing Association) trials for the Olympic Games. I've known you since you were so high and I think they've got it all wrong.' He went on to ask if anyone had set up a fund for me; a local councillor was apparently setting up a fund for road building, so somebody ought to do something for me!

Another time an old lady approached me when I was out training with Vicente in the park. 'I'm so sorry to disturb you,' she said politely, 'but I just wanted to shake your hand. I want you to know that I support you and that you're doing the right thing. Keep fighting. I just had to shake your hand.' And then she went on her way as if I had just done her a great honour.

It was the same story if we went out to any public place. Vicente and I have both been Manchester United supporters since our childhood and were proud to receive a telegram from Alex Ferguson and the team on our wedding day. In September we were invited to the European Cup match against Barcelona. As we made our way to our seats in the grandstand, fans everywhere turned round to welcome us. 'Go on, Diane!' 'Stay in there and fight.' 'We're all behind you,' they were calling. We were amazed and overwhelmed by these displays of support from people we had never met.

There was also support from other Christians that meant a lot. Shortly after Vicente's trip to Lisbon for the opening of the 'B' sample, we went to my brother's church in Didsbury. At the end of the service the minister said, 'I see we have Diane and Vicente here. Would you like to come to the front?'

Normally church is a personal and private thing for both of us. We were feeling particularly vulnerable at the time so were naturally apprehensive about what was going to happen. As we stood at the front the minister began to pray while two of the congregation laid their hands on us. He asked God to give us strength to get through the ordeal we were facing and we felt ourselves surrounded by the prayers of the whole church. Although we had our eyes closed, I know both of us had tears rolling down our cheeks as we stood there. The minister afterwards apologised if he'd caused us any embarrassment, but in fact it had been a moving experience for us both. As we were leaving, some of the church members stuffed pieces of paper in our hands which turned out to be prayers and psalms to encourage us.

I would be lying if I said that my faith stood rock solid throughout the whole ordeal. My mother would say, 'Never lose faith in God. He won't give you more than you can handle.' But I had lost some of my faith. It was difficult to comprehend why this should have happened to me. As a Christian I wasn't frightened of dying, but this was something different. I was still reading the Bible but I couldn't find any comfort in it. Nothing in my religion could explain the trial I was suffering. At one point, some time before the hearing, I even considered consulting a clairvoyant. 'He can tell me if we're going to win or not,' I thought. It was the endless waiting and not knowing that was unbearable, I needed an answer for my own sanity. The clairvoyant was highly recommended by a friend of Lesley's (Vicente's secretary). She knew of two top British athletes who had consulted him and his predictions had come true. It was a measure of my desperation that I was prepared to consider something that went against everything in my faith. I believe in God and I know that my future is in his hands but I needed some answers. I needed to be able to understand what was happening to me. Even my mother, who has always been strong in her Christian beliefs, said, 'If you feel that strongly about it maybe you should see this clairvoyant.' I was surprised at her response, but I was her daughter and she could see I was suffering badly, she wanted whatever was best for me.

I thought about the decision for weeks and weeks but I knew I wasn't settled within myself. Joy Williams, Christians in Sport Secretary and Special Projects Manager, with whom I am friendly, came to see me and I explained my dilemma. She said, 'I'm sure I can appreciate to some extent how you must be feeling, but I think you should just keep the faith. Trust in God and in what he's trying to do.'

'I know that,' I replied, 'but I just don't think it's fair. It may be selfish of me to say I demand an answer, I need to know why it's happening, but that's exactly how I feel.'

There were no simple answers. When you had a bad race you could put it down to something, but I couldn't find any reason in my faith for what was happening. It was too much to make sense of. I had lived an honest life and kept my faith but now I felt wronged, let down, slapped in the face. All the same, I still relied heavily on God to get me through the days and weeks. My faith had taken a hard knock but I didn't ever stop praying. My prayers weren't, 'Please let us win the case', because I believe God's will must be done anyway; I prayed only for us to get through it all – Vicente and I as a married couple, and my family, because in different ways we had all suffered.

The day of the hearing drew close – 13 December, the judgement day I'd waited for for so long. As it got nearer, my confidence that we would win grew stronger. We had put in hundreds of hours of work, we had delved into every aspect of the case and consulted the best medical experts, I'd been through tests of every kind and Vicente and Tony Morton-Hooper, our solicitor at Mishcon De Reya, had left no stone unturned; we were ready.

At the beginning of December we met with our medical and legal experts for a two-day briefing of our case. It was the first time we had met our barrister, Edwin Glasgow QC. Tony opened the meeting but was soon stopped by the barrister. 'Sorry to interrupt, Tony, you are running the show, but I would like to say a few words.' One hour later he was still talking! It was the longest interruption I'd ever heard but it was worth hearing. He began by saying, 'I'll make it clear now, we will win and we will win with a clear case and not a technicality. If this case had gone to court the IAAF and BAF would not have lasted two minutes.'

Edwin Glasgow was a leading barrister and gave us total

confidence, Tony was the backbone of our defence, often working late into the night to find new evidence, never content that enough had been done. Dr John Honour, Head of the Middlesex Hospital laboratory, was the backbone of our medical case. Dr Malcolm Brown, the BAF's own medical officer, had supported me from the very start. His involvement was at a personal cost: it lost him a place on the IAAF medical commission.

Later that evening in London, we went to see the film *Miracle on 34th Street* to try and escape for a couple of hours. It was about an old man who actually believes he is Santa Claus and finds himself in court, forced to prove his claim in order to avoid being sent to a mental institution. It was honesty against corruption, the individual against the system, with Santa Claus standing for the voice of the innocent. Vicente asked me afterwards if I thought Primo Nebielo, President of the IAAF, believed in Santa Claus.

Christmas was approaching but we had bought no presents and sent no cards. There was only one gift we were interested in that year: the hearing to finally tell the world the truth that I was innocent. The last few days dragged by painfully slowly, broken only by constant phone calls from the press. As the day approached, every paper ran daily bulletins speculating on what the verdict would be. There was hardly an athlete or medical expert left in Britain who hadn't been asked their opinion. We were back inside the pressure cooker. The hearing would be a media circus and I started to try and prepare myself. Since the day I'd stepped off the plane from Vancouver almost four months before, I hadn't faced the cameras and reporters. My only contact with the media in that time had been through studying it as my degree subject.

We left for London two days before the hearing to avoid anyone finding out where we were going to stay. Only hours after we drove away from our house, the first journalist was knocking on the door. We checked into a Kensington hotel under the name of Leiva, which was Vicente's father's name. The hearing was to be held at the Bloomsbury Crest Hotel near Euston station so we were far enough away to feel safe from the press.

Both of us were awake early on Tuesday, 13 December. It had been a sleepless night, each of us lying silently in bed, not wanting to wake the other. Now the day had come we wanted events to get moving as soon as possible. We had waited four months for this day to dawn, our hearts were full of hope that at last there would be light at the end of a long dark tunnel. In two days our fate would be decided – innocent – and we could start to rebuild our lives, or guilty – which would mean the unthinkable: a four-year ban from athletics and the nightmare continuing.

Inside I felt anxious, nervous and very frightened, but to the outside world I had to preserve the appearance of being composed and rational, as if it was just another normal day. The night before, leaving Tony's offices, I'd wanted to run up and hug him, to say, 'Tony, I'm relying on you, you're all I have.' I didn't, of course, we didn't even shake hands, we just smiled and said 'Good luck', then he disappeared, hands full of blue Mishcon De Reya folders as usual.

Vicente was up first and went out to buy some breakfast to eat in our room. He also bought the newspapers. My picture was all over the back pages but, as usual, I avoided reading them. We had a light breakfast of cheese, fresh bread, orange juice and yogurt, then got ready to travel to our solicitor's offices at Southampton Row.

The hearing started at 11 am sharp and well before that time we were travelling in a convoy of three taxis through the London traffic to the hotel. Vicente and I shared a taxi with Dr Malcolm Brown and our barrister, Edwin Glasgow. The others who made up our team were Tony Morton-Hooper and our three medical witnesses, Dr John Honour, Professor Howard Jacobs and Professor Gruneberg.

We were aware this was an important occasion, perhaps the most important day of our lives, and Vicente and I were both dressed formally, he in a dark green suit and me in a grey check jacket and skirt. I was conscious that it was the first time people had seen me since the day I had stepped dazed and bewildered off the airplane on 24 August. This time I wanted to look smart, not for anyone else, but for my own self-confidence.

As we drove up to the hotel doors, we could see the expected swarm of cameras and reporters waiting to meet us. I was the first to get out of the taxi, then Vicente and I held hands as we walked through the middle of the crowd. Microphones and camera lenses were thrust at us and reporters were shouting, 'Diane! Diane! This way. Any comments? Are you confident?' We just smiled and nodded and made our way inside the doors.

The press couldn't crowd in on us as they were kept behind a rope protecting the route to the door. It was one of the few things the BAF had managed to do right, we joked as we walked in. Our mood was nervous but positive. We were making jokes to relieve the tension.

We were shown into a small side room to await the start of the hearing. There was a window flooding the room with light. We sat down at a table laid with a jug of water and cups for tea or coffee. Somewhere in an identical side room on the other side of the building, we knew the BAF side were also making themselves ready. It was the first time we had met Professor Gruneberg, a microbiologist who was going to testify on the effect of bacteria in samples. Dr Honour and Professor Jacobs were there as our experts in the field of analysing steroids. I turned to Professor Jacobs and said, 'I never would have believed that one day I'd be sitting around a table with so many eminent people.' He laughed loudly and Edwin Glasgow said, 'Nor did I!'

Finally we were called in for the hearing. It was a surprisingly small room with the panel of five seated at the front and two tables at right angles facing each other to make a horseshoe formation. We sat at one table with the BAF side facing us. There was no formal seating plan and I found myself between Vicente and Malcolm Brown.

The whispering and scraping of chairs died down. It was about to begin. I looked at the faces of the five-strong panel. The chairman Martyn Lucking, Al Guy, Joslyn Hoyte-Smith, Chris Carter and Walter Nicholls. Somehow I'd reached this position where these people had the power to judge me, to say whether I was guilty or innocent of a crime I knew I hadn't committed. Three of them – Lucking, Hoyte-Smith and Carter – were former athletes themselves. Walter Nicholls was a solicitor and an official with the Northern AAA. Al Guy was a member of the IAAF technical committee. Linford Christie speaking on the *Breakfast with Frost* TV programme a week before had said that Martyn Lucking had once told him 'that all athletes are guilty until proven innocent'. Linford felt I had little chance of winning the hearing. After the introductions, the chairman, Martyn Lucking, opened proceedings and invited the BAF side to speak first. BAF's QC, Mr Pannick, started to speak. My hearing was finally underway and it all felt so unreal.

The line that the BAF were taking soon became crystal clear, it was hard-hitting and uncompromising. They had decided to ridicule the importance of all the flaws in the testing procedure. Chain of custody, the state of the sample, the disregard of normal doping regulations – none of these things mattered, they said, the only point worthy of attention was that the sample was positive and could only be explained by administering testosterone. Vicente and I held hands throughout Mr Pannick's long opening statement. Both of us felt we badly wanted to say that the case couldn't be reduced to one simplistic argument. Vicente was sighing heavily and shaking his head. I squeezed his hand, worried that he might lose control for a moment and try to interrupt. We'd been told that the opposition lawyers felt uncomfortable about fighting the case against me; it was a sad situation but they would have to go through the motions. Yet right at the start we were listening to them trying to discredit the entire basis of our case.

After Mr Pannick, it was Edwin Glasgow's turn to speak. As the hearing went on I began to notice something that worried me. None of the panel seemed to want to look in my direction or make eye contact with me. There were a couple of brief glances but nothing more. Proceedings went on through the long hours of the afternoon. The cramped room became increasingly hot and airless. It would have been so easy to close my eyes and dream of waking up somewhere far away. I was forcing myself to concentrate on what was being said. I knew my whole future was being decided in that room, I had to listen and follow.

Dr John Honour was talking. I felt the very thing we'd wanted to avoid was happening; the case was becoming very scientific, almost a battle between medical experts. Even though I'd been through it many times, it was hard for me to follow, I knew the panel would also be struggling to understand everything. They were teachers, ex-policemen and local GPs, not professors or heads of laboratories. John Honour was explaining an experiment he'd done only two days before the hearing. He argued that it showed why the bacteria had changed the character of the sample and caused such a high peak. The bacterial action had created either testosterone or something mimicking testosterone in the sample. The samples of urine tested by the Lisbon laboratory were so deteriorated that they should have been rejected. He said that he didn't see that anyone working in the field could draw any reliable conclusion about the presence of testosterone in such a sample. This was one of our key arguments, the most likely explanation of what had happened. Yet I felt the body language of the panel wasn't encouraging, they looked lost. The experts on the opposite table were shuffling their papers and whispering to each other. I began to worry that things weren't going our way.

During a break in proceedings, Tony took Vicente and me to one side. He admitted he too had misgivings. 'They've been avoiding you, Diane, they haven't been looking in your direction at all and that worries me.'

Yet despite such discouraging signs, I still clung to my faith in the hearing. In the face of all the serious doubts about the tests, I didn't believe we could lose. Listening to BAF's own expert, Dr Cowan, cross examined by our barrister, it was obvious that he too had reservations about some of things that had gone on in Lisbon. When Edwin Glasgow questioned him about the matter of chain of custody, for example, Dr Cowan had to admit that the 'B' test had gone ahead on an assurance that had never been honoured. Here, for the record, are his own words.

QC Glasgow   You asked for the chain of custody documents because you and the Professor (Beckett) are concerned to establish what has happened to the sample, not just that it is the right sample but where it has been and who has been handling it. That was why, was it not?

Dr Cowan   Maybe I can help there. At the start of the 'B' sample analysis, certainly in my laboratory I wished to get a statement from witnesses, but as far as they are concerned the chain of custody has been adequate. I do not see the purpose of a laboratory doing an analysis if subsequently it is shown that the chain of custody is inadequate.

QC Glasgow   Absolutely. We are absolutely at one, Doctor, I thought we would be. But when you asked whether those chain of custody documents existed, by which we mean the contemporaneous records made and the word used in

	the regulations is 'during', is it not? They are made during the handling, so there is no doubt they have to be made contemporaneously.
Dr Cowan	Yes.
QC Glasgow	Thank you. And when you were assured those documents existed, you believed what you were being told.
Dr Cowan	Indeed.
QC Glasgow	But it was a lie.
Dr Cowan	I could not comment on that . . . I had understood the documents were elsewhere and they had not been able to produce it.
QC Glasgow	And still have not.
Dr Cowan	I find that unacceptable.
QC Glasgow	If I may be permitted a comment, so do we. They still, to this day, have not produced what they told you they had got because they knew that you and the Professor would only conduct the 'B' experiment because you had been assured that the chain of custody documents were in existence. That is the truth, is it not?
Dr Cowan	Yes.

Dr Cowan was next questioned about his opinion of the Lisbon staff's laboratory practice and their general competence. We began with the 'B' test.

QC Glasgow	Where did they mix up the testosterone?
Dr Cowan	They started to actually open the bottle of testosterone in the laboratory. The analysis was going on and I said, 'I think it is better that you do not do that in here.'
QC Glasgow	They started to open the pure testosterone in order to look for a trace element, they actually physically opened that and were going to spoon it out in the laboratory where they . . .
Dr Cowan	They did not get as far as opening it.
QC Glasgow	They did not go as far? That is what they were going to do, was it?
Dr Cowan	Yes.

QC Glasgow	Doctor, but I think it is common ground between us, is it not, that a number of things that you found going on in Lisbon did not entirely satisfy you?
Dr Cowan	Yes.

Dr Cowan went on to expand on his reservations:

Dr Cowan	I felt there were one or two issues where I was not at all comfortable. I put it in my evidence. In particular the use of so-called proficiency standard sample where they could not convince me that they knew sufficiently about that sample to relate other things to it.
QC Glasgow	It did not convince you that they even knew enough about it. Those are your words.
Dr Cowan	That was my understanding, yes. I could not gloss over that.
QC Glasgow	What we were asking for, what everybody was asking the Portuguese lab for, was the selected ion traces for 417 and 342.
Dr Cowan	I do not dispute that.
QC Glasgow	With the greatest respect, may I just put it once again, Doctor. It is common ground between us, is it not, let us be blunt, the Portuguese have been thoroughly uncooperative in the investigation of this matter?
Dr Cowan	I have to agree with that.

Finally, when it came to the question of the sample degradation, there were further surprising admissions from Dr Cowan:

QC Glasgow	Going on then, you open the sample and you notice the smell. It was very obvious to you. Maybe you were the one closest to it at the time.
Dr Cowan	Yes.
QC Glasgow	But even the lab assistant who was doing the work did not apparently notice the . . .
Dr Cowan	That surprised me because when I said, 'Well

	didn't you notice it?', there were words like, 'No'. They did not seem to react to it, which I found surprising.
QC Glasgow	Then, notwithstanding the smell that you had to point out, you then had to ask whether the pH was being tested?
Dr Cowan	Yes.
QC Glasgow	They were not even aware of the fact that they had to do a pH test on a urine sample before they made the analysis and they were going to go ahead on the 'B' test in exactly the same way as they did the 'A' test, without any check on the alkalinity at all. That was your impression?
Dr Cowan	That was my impression.
QC Glasgow	We know, do we not, that on the 'A' test, because we have the record of it, they did not do an alkalinity test at all.
Dr Cowan	That is correct.
QC Glasgow	You had never done any analysis of a urine sample of this alkalinity before, had you? You had never tried to analyse one before this?
Dr Cowan	We have many years ago experience of having to analyse very poor samples. It is something that we try to avoid doing. Our first reaction is to refuse analysis of that sample. On occasions we have been pressed by the governing body, and with certain riders attached, we may be prepared to continue with the analysis. The first reaction is to say no.
QC Glasgow	You did actually tell the assembled team in this case that you would not have analysed this sample.
Dr Cowan	Yes.
QC Glasgow	Because they may convert from something else whereas obviously the purely synthetic things will not.
Dr Cowan	I made an additional report. I put in a report signed by Professor Beckett and myself at the time and they were the issues I was unhappy about. That is, I was not happy that we had a

sample of such a strong odour, in my view, and
therefore (it) had degraded. I was not happy
about a sample that ostensibly at the time of
sample collection had a pH of 5, let us say 5–6,
which at the time of the analysis now had a pH
closer to 9.

Given that these admissions were not coming from one of our
experts, but from the opposite side – from *the BAF's own
expert witness*, I could not see how anyone could still maintain
that administration of testosterone could be proved 'beyond
reasonable doubt'. Towards the end, it was my turn to give
evidence. Vicente had already given his account of the Lisbon
athletics meeting in June when I had taken the dope test, now I
was the last to speak. Despite my nerves, I was more than happy
to answer any questions. I'd waited so long for this, no one had
ever heard my version, I had a lot I wanted to say.

At first it seemed as if I wouldn't be given any opportunity to
speak. Our barrister, Edwin Glasgow, asked me just one real
question. 'Have you ever taken testosterone yourself or allowed
it to be administered to you?' I answered loud and clear, 'No.'

Mr Pannick addressed the panel. 'I think it would be pointless
to ask detailed questions, but of course you appreciate that the
case for the BAF has to be to the contrary, given the medical
evidence. I do not wish to ask any questions of Mrs Modahl.'

I wasn't totally surprised. Tony had told me earlier in the afternoon that I wouldn't be asked any questions by the prosecution.
They were taking the line that I had already been through enough
and it would be overstepping the mark to cross-examine me.
Vicente later said he felt this was a bad sign, as if the decision
had already been made and I'd been found guilty.

The chairman of the panel asked me a few questions, then Al
Guy, the IAAF representative, took over. He had been in charge
of doping control at the European Championships in Helsinki so
was part of the system I stood accused by. He began by asking
me about the altitude training in Mexico when I'd had the throat
infection. 'I suppose it would be fair to say it was a disaster,' he
said. I agreed.

'And this would certainly have put your programme back quite
considerably?' Again I admitted there had been a negative effect.

I had a feeling where this was leading. 'You indicated,' he went on, 'that you treated the Portuguese race basically as part of a build-up and that it was hard training during the build-up to the competition, two days off and you were beaten. I think you say somewhere that you went out with the idea of a further warm-up.'

'Small training. Yes and we did do that,' I answered.

Then his line of questioning became transparent. 'Malcolm (Brown) in his evidence earlier on did say that he felt the use of steroids was in the build-up period, in the heavy training. From what you say here, you tend to put this period into a build-up training period.'

I felt a flash of anger. Al Guy, a member of the panel, appeared to be suggesting that I had lost the effect of the training camp in Mexico and therefore used the Lisbon race as a training phase, a chance to make up the lost ground by using steroids. I decided to confront this implication head on.

'I understand what you are trying to say,' I told Mr Guy, 'but I must say it is absolutely ridiculous. During that period I am racing virtually every two weeks, to perhaps try and suggest that one would take a banned anabolic steroid in a period of so many races close together with a view to performing very well at those competitions . . . the chance of being tested or even randomly tested at that time must be one hundred per cent.'

'Please do not think I am suggesting anything,' he protested, 'but certain possibilities have been aired during the day and I think it is only fair that you should have the opportunity to come and comment on them here.' He then went on to underline the point that there was a twenty-minute gap after the race before I was notified of the drug test. Normal procedure, as I agreed, was to be told immediately.

'Did you take anything in the meantime between the notice and the end of the race?'

'No, not even water and it was a very hot day.'

'In your husband's evidence there is a feeling coming across that you may have been set up, spiked or something like that. Do you think this is a possibility?'

'It's impossible to answer that question,' I said shortly.

That was all. I shifted in my seat angrily. Again, I felt he was implying that in the twenty minutes after the race, I could have felt safe enough from doping control to take drugs. This ignored the fact that during the twenty minutes (a delay which was nothing to do with me) I stayed in the stadium or warm-up area the whole time in front of crowds of athletes and spectators. It also ignored the vital question of what I had to gain by using steroids straight after a race. Most disturbing of all, this cross-examination hadn't come from the BAF's barrister, which I might have expected, but from one of the panel.

Worse was yet to come. We still had to endure the closing summary for the BAF. It had grown dark outside and we were nearing the end of a long day. Despite the two or three breaks for drinks or sandwiches, I felt drained and suffocated by the cramped airless room.

The opposing QC, Mr Pannick, was making his closing state-ment which told a story I didn't recognise as connected to my own. He began by saying what, in his view, the case was not about. It was not about the leak to the Russians, it was not about whether the Portuguese laboratory practice was sub-standard, it was not about whether the sample should have been thrown in the bin, it was not even about whether I knowingly took steroids or how I could have done it.

Vicente and I were gripping each other's hands by this point, unable to stop the tears coursing down our cheeks. I couldn't believe what I was hearing. If the case wasn't about any of this, what was it about? If none of these things mattered what justice was there? The way Mr Pannick was brushing aside vital evidence seemed incredible to me. All the time he was talking directly to the panel, concentrating all his attention on them. I wanted him to turn and look me in the eyes to see if he really believed what he was saying.

He continued that there were only two realistic possibilities to consider: that the bacteria had affected the sample or that I had administered testosterone. Dr Honour's explanation – that the bacteria had reacted to create testosterone or something mimicking testosterone – they accepted as 'possible', but their medical experts 'thought it was highly improbable'. He went on to downgrade John Honour's evidence by saying that it dealt only in theory where Professor Brook and Professor James were dealing with 'practical reality'.

It was then Edwin Glasgow's turn. He made a long impassioned speech stating our case: first that the sample was degraded to the extent that it was unreliable, secondly that there was a failure of good practice in the laboratory and thirdly that both factors cast a real doubt on the fairness and reliability of the result. He asked why the benefit of the doubt should be given to the Portuguese when they had consistently got things wrong, refused to supply vital data or even to attend the hearing. Dr Cowan for the BAF had even admitted at the eleventh hour (we only got his statement the night before) that effectively the Portuguese didn't do the 'B' test, he did. He had to tell them to make a pH test, he had to tell them not to open naked testosterone in a place where they were going to carry out a test on my sample. He even admitted that he wouldn't have consented to the 'B' test going ahead, if he hadn't been misled regarding the existence of the chain of custody documents. And these were the people whose evidence the panel had to rely on to find me guilty!

Edwin Glasgow concluded with emotion: 'It is a thousand pities that the thing was leaked. It is a thousand pities the damage done to Diane's reputation, the extent to which this girl has been destroyed and probably will not ever recover. Enough damage has been done already. It has been done by incompetent, dishonest, bloody-minded people. They do not deserve your support, we do.'

It was over. But had we won or lost? I didn't know. The panel had seemed cold and wouldn't look in my direction. I felt as if they weren't interested in the real issues. Chris Carter had asked some sensible questions, as had the chairman, Martyn Lucking. Joslyn Hoyte-Smith had remained silent, though as a former athlete I'd hoped she would be able to understand my situation. Walter Nicholls was inscrutable. Al Guy had seemed intent on rescuing the BAF's case whenever it was in trouble. At one point Dr Cowan had been forced to admit, under cross-examination, that if a sample in the same state of deterioration as mine had arrived at his lab in London, he wouldn't have tested it because it would be unreliable. Al Guy then interrupted to ask if, regardless of the deterioration, Dr Cowan believed there had been administration of testosterone. Cowan agreed and once again the BAF's experts had been hauled back to what they said in their reports, with the help of a member of the panel.

Yet I still clung to the belief that they must see the truth and find me innocent. The charge that I had taken drugs had to be proved beyond 'reasonable doubt' and there were so many reasons to doubt. As we were leaving, one of the panel, Chris Carter, seemed to wave at Vicente. Vicente said he had actually given him a 'thumbs up' sign. What did it mean? 'We believe you' or 'We're sending you back to hell'? Vicente and I left the room and neither of us could keep up the mask of outward calm any longer. I went into the nearest toilet and broke down. Vicente followed me in and we tried to comfort each other. When we returned to the main room Edwin Glasgow was packing away his papers. He turned to me with a look of deep sympathy and said, 'I did my best for you, love.' That was when I knew we had lost.

The verdict

The next morning the two of us sat sick and lonely in our hotel room waiting to hear the decision. The waiting seemed to go on for eternity. We had been told that the verdict would reach us early in the morning. No news came. Whenever the phone rang we would pounce on it, only to hear the voice of a friend or relative asking what was happening. We rang Tony at the Mishcon De Reya offices over and over again. 'Anything?' 'Have you heard?' There was no news. The BAF lawyers promised Tony we would be the first to know.

The waiting went on through the long, tortuous hours of the morning. It was as if our agony was being stretched out like a piece of elastic to the point where we could bear no more and something must snap. At 1.25 pm the phone rang. I was in the bathroom trying to find something in my travel bag. I dashed back into the bedroom and threw myself down next to Vicente on the bed. We held the phone receiver between us. It was Tony's voice. 'I'm sorry but we lost.'

The world started to break up and slide away from me. Vicente was speaking but I couldn't find any words. Tony was saying that if we turned on the television, we would see Martyn Lucking reading the statement on the news. We'd been assured that we would hear before the media, how was it possible that it was on the TV screen even as the words reached us? We watched the pictures in stunned disbelief as Martyn Lucking read the statement in a slow, stumbling voice: 'Having heard all the evidence and considered all the documents, the committee was satisfied unanimously beyond reasonable doubt that a doping offence had been committed by Mrs Modahl. Accordingly she is ineligible to compete in the UK and abroad for four years from June 1994.'

Vicente had dropped the phone. I picked it up. Tony was still on the other end of the line. 'What do we do now?' I asked, desperately needing some hope to cling to. 'We fight on,' he said simply. I passed the phone back to Vicente. My body felt weak, as if I'd just been punched hard in the stomach. It was painful to breathe. I could see Lucking and other members of the panel as they'd appeared on the television screen. It was my life they were playing with, my innocent life. I let Vicente take me in his arms. I had nothing left to give. There were no words to comfort me. Vicente's face looked helpless, his eyes red and swollen. We felt as if we were alone in the entire world. The tears kept on coming until I was sobbing helplessly like a child.

Later I looked at myself in the mirror. 'How could I go on?' I asked my reflection. It was like being caught in an endless circle of torment. Again I was branded a cheat, again I knew it was a lie, again I had to drag myself off the floor and try to find an answer. I had gone into the hearing with such expectancy and hope, sure at last that the truth would be heard above the rumours and accusations. Now all kinds of disturbing questions started to surface in my mind. Martyn Lucking, quoted in *The Independent* the next day, made the decision sound almost a formality. 'We held a preliminary hearing in October,' he said (although in fact no case details were discussed then) 'and there were very few points of contention when it came to the hearing. But we had to rubber stamp it all as it came through.'

My life as an athlete was ruined, my love for athletics had died, the reason to wake up in the morning had gone, I was half way in the grave. But first I had to face the gathering vultures. There was a press conference arranged by Tony and Mishcon's press officer for 3.30 pm. I felt in no emotional state to answer questions so we prepared a short written statement. Vicente also wanted the chance to say something; I argued against this at first, but he insisted. We were trying to act normally, considering what we were both going through, but it didn't take much for tension to boil over.

The press conference was to be held in a hotel. Ironically, it was only a stone's throw from where we'd been staying. Half the journalists in London had been searching for us and there we were, just a short distance down the road. We were smuggled in through a back entrance to avoid the press at the main door. To get to the press conference room we were led down some stairs, up in a lift and then through the kitchen. It was like the last act of a terrible farce.

The room was just the way I had expected. Row upon row of strange faces, microphones, television and press cameras. There was the whirr of shutters clicking and bulbs flashed in my eyes as we entered. I sat down, relatively calm. I didn't want to answer questions because I wanted to say my piece in my own way, not have the direction of the conference hijacked by reporters. I was still in shock; it was hard to comprehend that it had all come down to this bitter moment.

A hush had fallen in the room. The only sounds were the cameras and water being poured into a glass. Everyone was waiting for me to speak. It was as though the reporters were taking in that Diane Modahl – the person at the centre of all this – actually existed, that she had a voice of her own. But I wasn't going to rush or be forced to break off; when I spoke I wanted to be heard. I read out my statement in a voice that sounded stronger than I felt.

> I was informed by my solicitor at about 1.30 pm today of the decision of the BAF disciplinary committee. I am horrified at the decision – and at the prospect of the nightmare of the last four months continuing. I cannot accept BAF's decision, and will carry on fighting to clear my name because I know I am innocent. I sat through the whole of Tuesday's hearing, I listened to all the evidence. I felt sure that the committee would decide that there were many doubts raised about the reliability of my test results. I have never taken any banned substance. I have declared my innocence. I shall challenge the committee's decision and take my case to the Independent Appeal Panel.

I wanted to say much more. I wanted to say that the panel had lied to themselves and to me. What the hell had been going through their minds? What on earth were they thinking when they found me guilty?

Vicente and Malcolm Brown took it in turn to say their piece. I cast my eyes round the room and saw something that made my heart miss a beat. There, in between the wall of camera lenses and journalists, were the faces of my own mother and father. In that room they looked totally lost and numb with pain. I couldn't reach out to them or speak, I couldn't even acknowledge them, because I knew their presence was a potential time-bomb. Reporters from every national newspaper, TV and radio station were present in the room. If they'd known Diane Modahl's parents were standing right next to them there would have been a stampede to get their story.

When Tony had finished answering questions we all retired to a back room. I said, 'My Mum and Dad are in there! Can someone please bring them through?' Tony thought up a pretext to get them safely away, pretending that they were staff who worked for him. I'd put my parents off coming to the hearing because I was worried that they might be harassed by the media and the strain would be too much. After the verdict I'd tried to call them from the hotel room but now I understood why there had been no answer. It was hard to imagine what they went through in those few minutes, seeing the youngest daughter they were so proud of, sitting in front of the nation's press, once again publicly branded guilty and a cheat.

The day was 14 December 1994. There were only eleven days before Christmas but there was nothing for us to celebrate. We had put Christmas away on the shelf until the hearing was over. Now it would stay there collecting dust. Other people would be looking forward to the holiday, to wrapping presents, cooking the turkey, spending time with their family. We couldn't be with our loved ones because we didn't want to be pitied or to increase the pain they already felt. There was no Christmas present that anyone could give us that year because the one we'd so desperately longed for had been snatched away. Outside the hotel, people were heading home past London's brightly lit shop windows and street decorations. To us, the winter evening sky looked dark and hopeless.

Chapter 12

Going The Distance

Fight on. What else could we do? The newspaper headlines the next morning screamed, 'Cheated!' 'Guilty!' One paper said that I had betrayed my nation. I wanted to tell them it was the wrong way round – *they had betrayed me*. I had represented my country faithfully for eleven years as an athlete, now I was branded a liar and left out in the cold to die.

No matter what it took – our house, our livelihood, our peace of mind – we had to go on fighting until my name and reputation, as well as my husband's, were cleared. I had the right of appeal to an independent panel, chosen again by the BAF. We would take our case there, and then, if necessary, to the civil court.

There was only one problem. We were already amassing a huge debt in legal fees. To keep fighting we needed the financial resources to pay for lawyers and medical experts and build an even stronger case.

We met with our solicitor, Tony Morton-Hooper, at his offices the next day. There seemed to be only one option available to us: to sell our story. Rumours said that we had been offered large sums by tabloid newspapers. It was true, but we turned down the offers. If we were to tell our story, it had to be set out truthfully and without sensationalism. We had enough experience of the tabloid press to know we couldn't trust them to write it the way we wanted. Writing a book was the only answer.

Some reporters wanted us to fight on but said that if we sold our story we were the lowest of the low – it proved our motive was money rather than the truth. How did they expect us to continue the fight for the truth? We were two individuals up against the might of the BAF and IAAF, sporting bodies with multi-million pound backing. No one had ever won an appeal against the BAF before. Our story was the only weapon we had left to continue the fight. It was also time that the world heard it from our point of view.

We left London to return home. A few days before we had driven south, full of hope, confident that our nightmare would soon be over. Now as we returned, our hopes were shattered and our lives once again thrown into turmoil. Most of all we dreaded the prospect of Christmas. Normally we looked forward to the holiday with high excitement. The year before, Vicente had taught me to cross-country ski in Norway. The snow had been three feet deep outside the family house where we stayed and the countryside was a fairy tale landscape.

We knew at this time of year everyone would be closing down their business and going home to celebrate with their families. For us it meant a yawning gap in our lives for three weeks. We couldn't celebrate, there was nothing *to* celebrate, we wanted to get straight back to fighting this monstrous decision. Yet we knew that was impossible. The telephone was our lifeline and for the Christmas and New Year holiday period it would stop ringing. We couldn't dial Mishcon De Reya and ask Tony what was happening. He had a wife and children that he needed to spend time with. The prospect of life coming to a halt scared us.

The previous evening in London, unable to sleep, desperation and despair had taken over. Vicente suddenly suggested we should stage a protest run from Manchester to London, arriving on Christmas Day to deliver a letter to the Minister of Sport. I said I was in no state to run but I was willing to go on hunger strike to show the world that I was innocent and that the truth had been denied me. We were both equally convinced by our own ideas and equally unconvinced by each other's. In the end I said, 'You run to London and I'll sit here and have my hunger strike.' We can laugh at ourselves looking back, but it is a measure of how desperate we felt at the time that we were both deadly serious. In the end we phoned Tony and asked for his opinion. He very diplomatically pointed out that, although the idea could work, it would be seen as a publicity stunt and used against us in the appeal.

We still had the daunting prospect of Christmas and New Year to survive. A few days before Christmas, Vicente went into a travel agency and booked a ten-day holiday to Thailand. It was a surprise for me, although one I was half expecting. I felt guilty; we didn't have the money to go on holiday, we hadn't even paid our legal bills, but in order to survive we needed to do something to get away from 'the case'. For four months we'd been living on the edge of a precipice, and when the verdict was announced we both knew there was a danger that one of us might tip over the edge. We had reached the limits of our endurance. Normally a Christmas holiday in Thailand would have been the trip of a lifetime, but in our case it was just somewhere to get as far away as possible.

We did our best to salvage something from the ashes of 1994, but fate seemed to be against us from the start. We were due to travel to Thailand the day before Christmas Eve but at Manchester airport the flight was delayed for five hours. Our troubles weren't over when we arrived: British Airways admitted that they'd lost our luggage. We were left with just our hand luggage and the clothes we stood up in. It was five days before our clothes reached us and the only compensation we got was enough money to buy a cheap pair of trousers each. It was hard to believe, our ill luck seemed to follow us across the world. We decided that 1994 was the wrong year for us.

We passed Christmas Eve watching a video and eating chocolate and crisps instead of the smoked lamb ribs we'd have feasted on in Norway. Christmas Day we avoided altogether by taking a boat trip to the floating market where we bought sweet bananas and Coca-Cola. Later we visited a snake farm and watched a bizarre show where the snakes popped balloons in their mouths and the trainer squeezed their jaws to show us the venom. Vicente had to accompany me to the bathroom later because I was convinced there was a green snake hanging from the ceiling.

Good days like this – of laughter and forgetfulness – were precious, but they fought against the underlying tide of despair. One afternoon I sat on the beach looking at the endless blue sweep of Siam Bay. Its beauty only made my own sadness more stark. I bent my head and cried for a long time, my body shaking with grief. Vicente did his best to comfort me but there was nothing he could say. I had lost too much. Even if I eventually won the case how could I ever return to athletics? Running had been my life. Something pure and innocent had been taken away from me and it could never be restored again.

My nights were broken by terrifying nightmares. There was one recurring dream where I watched myself die several times. I was walking through a forest. My parents and Vicente were there and I knew I was spending my final hours with them. The path I followed led to my own execution which was to be administered by a lethal injection. I was protesting but no one listened to me. Then the scene changed and I was being chased through the trees by an angry mob. They were shouting and threatening me. In my terror, I must have been struggling or calling out because I woke up to find Vicente shaking me in bed.

The dreams reflected the darkness of my waking hours. Life was too painful to bear and it often seemed pointless to carry on. I felt guilty for the suffering I was causing my parents and my endlessly caring husband. There were times I seriously contemplated suicide. Once, I sat upstairs in our bedroom at home with a knife on the floor in front of me for over an hour. What held me back from taking my life was not my own will to go on but the knowledge of what my death would do to those I left behind. It was too unfair. I couldn't inflict it on my poor Mum and Dad. I couldn't leave Vicente alone because I knew how much he loved me.

The worst of my twenty-eight years on earth – 1994 – finally passed as all years must. The Queen had described 1993 in her Christmas speech as an 'Annus horribilis'. For us there were no words capable of summing up the year we had just endured. But what could we dare to hope for in 1995? We saw the New Year dawn in Thailand, at a gala dinner in the Cha-Am resort. A banquet was held in the hotel garden with tables groaning under mountainous plates of lobster, crab, oysters and salad. Some of the local Thai people did their best to entertain us with English songs performed with an endearing disregard for the right tune and intonation. There were a table of British holidaymakers close to us who we noticed casting glances in our direction. 'The Modahl Affair' had even reached the pages of the *Bangkok Post* so we guessed that they probably recognised me. Thankfully, they respected our wish to be alone.

When midnight struck one of them approached us and insisted that we share a glass of champagne with them. Perhaps it was their way of wishing us a better future. Vicente and I raised our glasses and looked into each other's eyes.

'Happy New Year.'

'Let's be strong and fight.'

A cascade of balloons was unleashed from somewhere. People were cheering and kissing each other, fireworks lit up the sky exploding in showers of green, red and gold. A year had passed and a new one was dawning. What did it hold for us? More waiting, more experiments and tests, more working, hoping, praying, more pain, sleepless nights and enduring the crushing weight of despair? Or would the dark sky finally be lit by something miraculous? Would the world finally come to its senses and see that I was the innocent victim of a terrible mistake and an unjust system.

On the flight home from Thailand I felt a sense of dread at returning to face the wreckage of our lives and the seemingly endless struggle to prove my innocence.

Only a week later we were back in the world of samples, tests and trials. This time, however, some of the results were startling. On 7 January I gave a series of three urine samples after an intensive session of hill training where I ran until I was almost on my knees. The idea was to simulate the kind of hard training I'd done at the stadium in Lisbon before giving a sample. Then we would reproduce the same kind of conditions in which the samples were kept for two days in the San Antonio stadium complex in order to discover the effects of deterioration. I gave three different samples within four hours of the training session. They were then left at room temperature, open to direct sunlight from Saturday to Monday morning. The first sample – given after one hour – changed its pH value from 5 to 9 (just like my samples in Lisbon) while the other two samples surprisingly remained at pH 5. The obvious conclusion was that the changes brought about when bacteria grow in urine are so unpredictable that no reliable results can ever be based on them. When tested, a range of 15–20 types of bacteria were found in the samples, most of which had the ability to convert to testosterone.

The following month, February, it was Vicente's turn. He volunteered to undergo tests of a kind which every fibre in his body revolted against. Under the supervision of Dr John Honour and staff at Middlesex Hospital, Vicente took injections and oral doses of testosterone. John Honour had agonised for weeks over the ethics of conducting the tests but the final decision was left with Vicente. The aim was to test the IOC's and Professor Manfred Donike's theory that the metabolites – a by-product of natural testosterone – would be hardly visible if the dose was taken within hours of giving a sample. Vicente had never taken a banned drug in his life, it was disgusting and upsetting to subject himself to the tests but the sacrifice was worthwhile if it helped to prove my innocence. The results couldn't have been more conclusive. After two hours the metabolites had risen by six or seven times their normal level. They were tested every two hours and the peak remained and only started to diminish eight hours later. In my case the metabolites had been suppressed to the point where they were hardly visible. Donike had claimed this was because the drug had been taken within hours of giving the sample, but Vicente's tests had proved this theory utterly wrong.

A few weeks before, a positive result of a different kind had promised to change our lives. I was going to have a baby. We were both thrilled and excited as we looked forward to October when the baby was due. Yet it was impossible to echo the old cliché that our happiness was complete. We didn't want our baby to be born at a time when our lives were shattered and still in need of so much repair. Much as we tried, it was hard to feel real elation – we had known too much sadness. Our hopes and dreams had worn threadbare.

It wasn't until the spring that I felt the first tug of new life on my own. The midwife was crouching beside me on the sofa, holding an instrument called a foetal sonicaid to my stomach to let me hear the baby's heartbeat. She warned me that we had to be lucky – it depended on the position of the baby. I listened and suddenly, for a few seconds, I heard it, a continuous beat, loud and fast. I started laughing.

The midwife patiently explained I wouldn't hear it if I kept laughing. I managed to control myself and listened again. It was unmistakable. Beat–beat–beat–beat. A life growing inside me. Amazing. Marvellous. Impossible to describe in words. Vicente was away in Japan at the time working with his athletes. I so wanted him to be there to hear it. I wrote him a letter that night. 'Today I heard the best sound I have ever heard in my life . . .'

With the spring came another less welcome sound. The sound of a gun firing and spiked feet pounding up the track. The new athletics season had begun and for the first time since I was 13, it was starting without me. I watched the beginning of the first indoor meeting on television. After one race I couldn't bear to watch any more. I had to turn away and leave the room. Vicente didn't need to ask what was wrong. It tore me apart to see the life that had been taken away from me. I went upstairs and lay on my bed, asking myself again, was it worth going on? Did it make any difference? Nothing had stopped. The gun fired, the athletes ran, there was a winner and there were losers, then another race. I wasn't needed. Nobody missed me or mentioned my name.

In April Vicente took his athletes away on a training camp in Albuquerque, New Mexico, to prepare. It was another marker to the early season which normally would have involved me. We avoided the subject during the weeks beforehand. Vicente once suggested that I could come out for a week but I made the excuse that it wouldn't be good for the baby. Both of us knew the real reason was that I didn't want to be around other athletes training, sharing jokes and getting keyed up in anticipation of the season ahead. I didn't want to be the unwanted guest at the party, spoiling the atmosphere and forcing everyone to walk on broken glass whenever I entered a room.

Vicente went without me. He telephoned me every day from Albuquerque and I did my best to encourage him, but I could tell from his voice that he was longing for me to come out and join them. There was no joy for him in the trips away any more, he felt that it was almost like a betrayal and his place was beside me at home. In the end I went for the last week and the other athletes accepted me naturally into the group. But it was something I did for my husband, I knew I would rather be elsewhere.

Only four days after our return, Vicente had to pack his bags and go away again. It began to dawn on me that this was what it would be like, him jetting off round the world to prepare his athletes for important races, whilst I stayed at home. I wanted him to carry on with his work but I hated him going away. Up to that point my life had been totally absorbed by athletics, now I realised how limited my horizons were. I found myself alone with no companions but my despair and depression.

On good days I was buoyed up by the hope that the appeal

would have to clear me. We now had such a strong case it appeared unanswerable. So much had happened to strengthen our evidence since the BAF hearing in December. Then we had argued that the degradation of the sample was the likeliest explanation of my positive test. Dr John Honour had been frantically conducting experiments right up to the day before the hearing in an attempt to show how a deteriorated sample could create a false result. Despite the fact that the onus of proof wasn't on us, our case had been rejected. This time was different; we had some of the world's leading experts in the field of sample deterioration lining up to support our argument that, in the right conditions, bacteria *can and does* create a false positive test. The American Professor Paul Talalay was the Carl Lewis of his field, a distinguished professor of pharmacology and molecular sciences. He was joined by Dr Robert Owen, a toxicologist from the Cancer Research Institute, Heidelberg. Together they had published several hundred papers on the subject of steroid conversion. They maintained that no difficult chain reaction was needed for bacteria to produce a conversion to testosterone. Only one reaction was necessary and they could prove it had happened before. Neither of them had ever met me but both offered to speak in our case because they felt a grave injustice had been done.

In Britain, meanwhile, Professor Rod Bilton, Head of Biomolecular Sciences at John Moores University, published an article in the *Lancet* medical journal, adding his voice to our cause. Unless urine samples are stored correctly, refrigerated and in sterile containers, he warned that contaminated bacteria can transform steroid naturally found in urine to testosterone. In plain language that meant a female athlete could be found guilty because of a 'false positive' result.

It wasn't only our own experts who believed that a serious error had been made. Tony and his assistant James Hardy contacted scientists around the world and in confidence asked for their opinion on whether a urine sample, degraded to a level of pH 9, could be reliably tested, and whether they could help us on the complex science of steroid conversions in urine.

Without exception they were horrified that a test had been performed on such a degraded sample. Many helpfully suggested names of scientists who had the greatest understanding of this type of conversion. We soon discovered it was an obscure area of science and most of the research had been done many decades ago.

Our enquiries enabled us to identify and contact the small number of scientists who really knew something about the subject and could support what Dr Honour had said at the December hearing, even though the BAF's experts had dismissed his argument and had persuaded the Disciplinary Committee to do likewise.

We felt we now had all the evidence to support what we had maintained all along: that the result was due to a degraded sample and the analysis had been fatally flawed. We were ready and – with our baby due in the autumn – eager to clear the record as soon as possible. The only obstacle was that the BAF seemed to be dragging their feet over the appeal. Astonishingly and out of the blue, their lawyers suggested that the remainder of my 'B' sample should be subjected to further limited tests before any appeal could be heard. This might have been promising if it hadn't been for the fact that they were suggesting the tests should be carried out by Dr Barbosa in Lisbon – at the same lab and by the same staff which we believed were responsible for so many mistakes in the first place! Furthermore, the last time Vicente had seen the 'B' sample, it was left unsealed on a table in the Lisbon lab. How did we have any guarantee that any of my original 'B' sample *still existed*, let alone know what condition it was in? Yet again the BAF expected to make all the rules of the game and then asked why we didn't want to play along. We had requested as early as the previous September an independent test on the 'B' sample at the IAAF laboratory in London; what was to be gained from another test in Lisbon eight months later? In any case, why hadn't it been thought necessary before the hearing at which BAF's experts and the committee itself declared themselves certain enough of the results to find me guilty? We could only guess that our opponents were worried and wanted to delay the appeal to give them more time.

After long delays and many letters to the BAF's lawyers, one of which took as long as two months to receive a reply, the date for the appeal was set for 24–25 July. Our case seemed watertight, surely it was impossible that the truth could be ignored a second time? At the same time I was under no illusions as to what we were up against. No athlete had ever won an appeal against the BAF. I knew no one wanted to accept that a mistake could have been made. It was the life of one athlete against the whole credibility of the national and international governing bodies in athletics.

In my best moments I sometimes glimpsed a future where I would get back on the track and achieve the dreams that had been snatched away from me at the height of my career. I knew it was Vicente's heartfelt desire to give me the chance to run again and he would do anything to make it possible. But in my deepest self I no longer believed in those dreams. Regardless of whether we eventually won the fight for my innocence, we had already lost. We could never go back to what we had before 24 August 1994. That day had changed my life irrevocably and I was no longer the same eager, exuberant and trusting athlete who had claimed a place in the world's top four only the year before.

Since the age of 11 I had been involved in athletics, Vicente for even longer. Throughout our careers we had practised what we'd preached: honesty, sheer hard work, dedication and commitment. We had looked forward to the day that our own children might pull on a vest to run for Sale Harriers and we could stand on the sidelines to support them. We didn't know if we wanted that day any more. We had trusted the system and the system had taken our fruit and discarded us like the unwanted peel. All we had left was our determination to fight on and the knowledge of the truth in our hearts.

Over and over again I have asked myself and asked God why it happened. Why should I have been the victim of an injustice so cruel and relentless that it has robbed me of almost everything I hold dear in life. There has been no answer to my question, only the hope that some day in the future the clouds will part and everything will look differently. Whilst in Albuquerque I read a poem that expressed this hope and gave me an enormous amount of comfort. This book is written while Vicente and I are still going through our darkest hour. Maybe one day we'll look back and say that God carried us through, even when we felt utterly and desperately alone.

FOOTPRINTS

One night I dreamed a dream.
I was walking along the beach with my Lord.
Across the dark sky flashed scenes from my life.
For each scene, I noticed two sets of footprints in the sand,
One belonging to me and one to my Lord.
When the last scene of my life shot before me
I looked back at the footprints in the sand
and to my surprise,
I noticed that many times along the path of my life
there was only one set of footprints.
I realised that this was at the lowest
and saddest times of my life.
This always bothered me
and I questioned the Lord
about my dilemma.
'Lord, you told me when I decided to follow You,
You would walk and talk with me all the way.
But I'm aware that during the most troublesome
Times of my life there is only one set of footprints.
I just don't understand why, when I needed you most,
You leave me.'

He whispered, 'My precious child,
I love you and will never leave you,
Never, ever, during your trials and testings.
When you saw only one set of footprints,
It was then that I carried you.'

Margaret Fishback Powers

Chapter 13

Towards The Dawn

I began crossing off the days on the calendar to 24 July, the date set for the BAF independent appeal panel to hear my case. If my appeal was turned down – and no British athlete had ever succeeded before me – there would be no other choice but to take the battle to the civil courts.

Throughout the case the IAAF held the prospect of a further test over my head. Since the B test, we had repeatedly asked for an adequate portion of my sample to be returned and had our requests flatly rejected. After the December hearing, Tony had written, on 20 January 1995, to the IAAF through the BAF, asking them to confirm that there was a balance of the B sample available and, if so, making the following offer:

> the remainder of the sample can be handed over to the safe custody of Dr Cowan at his accredited laboratory in London pending final agreement between the parties' experts as to the details of the laboratory tests to be carried out on the remainder of the sample with a view to clarifying, if not resolving, some of the scientific issues which arise in this case.

No reply from the IAAF was ever received, not even confirmation that some remainder of my B sample still existed.

Before the appeal a meeting of experts was set for 20 and 23 June to see if there could be any agreement on the scientific issues. By an astonishing coincidence, on 6 June we were told that the further test was to take place in Portugal on 22 June – sandwiched right between the two dates and guaranteed to ensure maximum disruption. Since the BAF have never disclosed any of their correspondence with the IAAF on my case, we shall never know whether this was truly a coincidence or not.

Neither Dr John Honour nor Professor Simon Gaskell, two of our key experts, could be present as witnesses in Portugal at such late notice. The IAAF were informed of this but replied that they were unable to rearrange the date and the test must go ahead. Then, out of the blue, they performed a staggering U-turn. Two days before the scheduled test, we were told it would *not* take place. IAAF have never given a satisfactory explanation as to why it was cancelled, although lack of co-operation from the Portuguese was strongly rumoured in the press.

Even at the time of the appeal, the IAAF were again threatening a further test to clarify the situation. Two questions bothered me. First, if they were so sure of my guilt on the evidence they already had from Lisbon, why did they need any further test? Second, if they had nothing to hide why could the test not take place at Dr Cowan's IOC accredited laboratory in London? Dr Cowan had already given evidence that he was sure I was guilty so could hardly be accused of bias towards me!

The most galling part was the IAAF's public statements which tried to suggest a benign neutrality. Ten days before the appeal, the following came out on the Press Association wires:

> The IAAF today confirmed they had agreed to a request from the British Federation for a third analysis . . . 'if they request it, then we have nothing against it,' IAAF General Secretary Istvan Gyulai said. 'If they believe that further information can be obtained from it which would dismiss any doubts that they may have, then they can go ahead. The only concern was whether this would create a precedent, but to be fair to the extreme is more important for the IAAF.

The meeting between experts from both sides went ahead on 20 June. At this, BAF's side argued they needed to see proof that a badly stored urine sample could produce an increased testosterone ratio of its own accord. Of course there was no proof since no one was interested in badly-stored urine samples and no papers existed on the subject. Again, I felt they were effectively reversing the burden of proof, asking me to prove my innocence, as opposed to them proving my guilt. It was not enough that we had produced some of the world's leading experts in the field of steroid transformation who backed my case. Although BAF's experts were eminent scientists none of them was expert in this particular field.

The meeting effectively threw down a challenge, which Professor Gaskell, Professor Owen and Professor Bilton, unknown to me, decided to take up. In the limited time available they would each do some laboratory work on the theory.

The result was a dramatic breakthrough. Just over a week before the appeal, Simon Gaskell rang to say that he had *proved* that poorly-stored samples could produce a dramatic increase in T/E (testosterone to epitestosterone) ratio. (His protocol for the experiments was carried out by Dr Brian Brownsey at the Tenovus Institute for Cancer Research in Cardiff.) His experiments, at the University of Manchester Institute of Science and Technology, took samples from two female athletes, one after a long race, the other after playing tennis. Both of the samples were refrigerated and then tested for their T/E ratio. Both were well under the accepted limit of 6:1. He then took a portion of each of the samples and incubated them at 37°C (body temperature) for 72 hours. The samples were then retested. In one of the samples there had been a dramatic shift in the T/E ratio to over 30:1. My own sample had a ratio of 42:1. This was the most conclusive proof yet that such an extraordinary testosterone level could be caused by bacteria in a badly-stored sample. This exciting news brought with it an unwanted complication. On the Friday before the hearing, as we were preparing to travel to London, we heard that the BAF had asked for an adjournment in response to the 'new' evidence.

Further delay was unthinkable. our baby was due at the beginning of October and an adjournment might realistically mean waiting until the new year. There were fifteen people involved in our team alone, including internationally respected scientists whose diaries were booked up many months in advance. What troubled me even more was the thought that my health couldn't bear the strain of yet another postponement. I had suffered from high blood pressure and fainting fits during my pregnancy and we genuinely feared for the safety of our baby. While the taxi waited outside, we were holding urgent conversations with my consultant and GP, both of whom agreed to write letters warning that an adjournment might pose a serious risk to my health and that of our unborn child.

We boarded the train to London in a state of nervous anxiety, not knowing if the appeal would go ahead. BAF were arguing that they needed time to evaluate the research undertaken by Simon Gaskell. In fact they had been given five days to study the data and had turned down an invitation to go through the evidence with our team of experts before the appeal started.

The morning of the appeal, Monday 24 July, arrived with the crucial decision still to be made. I found it impossible to sleep the night before. Vicente was certain that this time we must win, but in my heart I couldn't bring myself to believe it. I had put my faith in the system once before and seen my hopes trampled in the dust, how could I rekindle the embers of that faith again? On rare occasions I looked into the future and imagined myself back on the track, hearing the crack of the gun and the crowd urging me on, but I quickly pushed such thoughts away; it was too dangerous to allow myself to believe in the end of the nightmare yet.

On Monday, the familiar chain of events unfolded again. The convoy of taxis through the London traffic, the press corps waiting outside and, finally, the cramped room where the appeal would be heard. I passed through each stage like a sleepwalker. At the December hearing I'd been nervous and hopeful, this time I felt like an outsider, listening to people discussing somebody else's life history. I had detached myself to a place far away where I couldn't be affected by all this. The three-strong appeal panel, chaired by Robert Reid, QC, and including Beryl Randle of the Midland Counties AAA and Gordon Wright, treasurer of Northern Counties AAA, first had to rule on the BAF's adjournment request. Robert Reid, looking every inch a judge peering at us over his spectacles, announced that they would need ten to fifteen minutes to come to a decision. Vicente looked tense while we waited; later he told me he'd been praying. ('If you don't let it go ahead for me, God, please do it for my wife.')

The panel returned and I held Vicente's hand while we awaited the decision. Briskly, Robert Reid announced that there would be no adjournment, the case had already gone on long enough and my health had to be taken into consideration. Round One had gone our way and set the pattern for the rest of the first day. Simon Gaskell revealed the results of his experiments with confidence and clarity, openly inviting the BAF scientists to come to his laboratory and examine the samples for themselves. What had been presented as a compelling theory by John Honour at the December hearing was now there for everyone to see in conclusive fact – that a deteriorated sample could give rise to greatly increased levels of testosterone.

Importantly, Dr Cowan said he believed that when the sample had been unrefrigerated in Lisbon, although the outside temperature was around 20°C, a sample inside an Envopak, inside a bag, in a closed room, could easily have risen above 37°C. The BAF side were unable to criticise the work of Professor Gaskell and his colleague, Dr Brian Brownsey; in fact when, at the end of the day, their experts belatedly asked to look at the data in more detail, they were complimentary about a professional, thorough and impressive piece of research.

The second day turned to look at other issues – the chain of custody, the competence of the Lisbon laboratory, the absence of metabolites and the question marks surrounding the T/E ratio. Vicente and I sat at the back throughout the proceedings, sometimes having to lean forward to catch what was being said. It underlined my feeling that I played only a supporting role in this courtroom drama, it was as if a system or a science was on trial rather than my own future.

Then abruptly – around three o'clock on Tuesday afternoon – it was all over. Robert Reid informed us that he wished to deliver the panel's verdict in writing and therefore hoped to announce it not later than Thursday. That meant anything between twenty-four and forty-eight hours of waiting. I wondered how we were going to survive in the meantime.

Back at Mishcon De Reya I wanted to say a word of personal thanks to every member of our team for their dedication and commitment on my behalf. Professor Paul Talalay had travelled from America to give evidence for the first time in a case of this nature because, as he told us, it was a moral issue where his conscience wouldn't let him rest. Others similarly had made considerable sacrifices of time and effort in order to support me. As I began to thank them all, my voice broke and tears welled up in my eyes. They had given everything they could; they were returning to their lives and, now it came to the waiting, Vicente and I were back on our own. No one said, 'We've done it' or 'We must win', we knew our case had been presented convincingly but now it was up to the panel.

That night I was distraught. Despite my sense of watching the proceedings from the outside, the tension of the two-day hearing had taken its toll on me. I felt I wanted to die; heaven had to be a better place than this. During the eleven months of my ordeal I'd contemplated suicide more than once. Now, if the verdict went against me once more, I felt I had nothing left to live for and no will to go on. I asked Vicente if I wasn't here, whether the legal bills could still be paid. Would I be running away from my responsibilities? I don't think he fully understood my meaning but he did his best to calm and reassure me. It would be all right in the end, he kept saying. I should think of the baby. I lay down on the bed afraid to close my eyes because I didn't want the morning to come.

I slept fitfully and awoke when Vicente went out for a run at six. The date was Wednesday 26 July, the day I would know my fate. It was torture staring at the four walls of our hotel room waiting for the phone to ring. Every time it rang my heart stopped, but each time it was a false alarm. So in the afternoon we went out, taking Vicente's mobile phone with us. We wandered towards Oxford Street and found ourselves outside the British Museum. Having checked that the mobile phone worked inside, we climbed the stairs to the Egyptian section on an upper floor to try and lose ourselves in gazing at the mummies and tombs. Even there, surrounded by relics of the ancient past, the unwelcome present intruded in the form of an autograph hunter who wanted to wish me luck.

On our way back to the hotel, the phone went at 4.45 pm. It was Tony telling us that the decision had been prepared and would be announced in the next half hour. The lethargy of the afternoon was suddenly replaced by frantic action as we hurried to get changed in readiness for the press conference. The phone went again around 5 pm. Vicente grabbed the mobile. There was a pause of a few seconds then he shouted, 'Haaa!' 'Ja!' ('Yes' in Norwegian), punching the air in triumph. There was no need to ask what the message was, Vicente's face crumpled in tears as I took the phone. Tony's voice on the other end of the line said, 'We've won.' He told us to come to Mischon's offices as soon as possible.

Vicente and I hugged each other, tears of relief and elation flowing freely. 'We won, we won,' we kept saying to each other, as if to try and let the marvellous truth sink in. I had been so successful in steeling myself for yet another blow that I hadn't prepared for victory at all. I rang my parents immediately to tell them the news. When my father answered the phone and heard the result I heard him call my mother's name, 'Lena! Lena! Lena!' – those were the only words he could say. Later, at Mishcon's offices, we read the appeal panel's ruling in full. It ran to eleven pages summarising the verdict on the main issues. On the question of chain of custody 'unsatisfactory features' were noted, namely the lack of contemporaneous documentation and the behaviour of the Lisbon staff who were 'less than frank' (a carefully worded euphemism) at the time of the B sample.

The panel's final summary stated:

When we take all the factors put before us together we come to the conclusion we cannot be sure beyond a reasonable doubt of Mrs Modahl's guilt. On the evidence before us there is a possibility which cannot be ignored that the cause of the T/E ratio in the samples of her urine was not that testosterone had been administered but that the samples had become degraded owing to their being stored in unrefrigerated conditions and that bacteriological action had resulted in an increase in the amount of testosterone in the samples. Mrs Modahl is therefore entitled to succeed in her appeal.

The rest of that day and the next were a blur of phone calls and press interviews. Where I had once turned down all requests from the media, I now felt I had some important things to say. I had been branded a liar and cheat in some quarters and, when I repeatedly protested my innocence, was put to the task of raising more than 'a reasonable doubt' about the findings. Yet I wanted to underline the fact that I pledged my full support to the BAF and IAAF in their efforts to stamp out drug abuse in sport. I had never criticised the entire dope testing system, I simply claimed that one laboratory in Lisbon had been badly at fault in their practices. For the good of sport and in order for athletes to have faith in the system, it was vital for the IAAF to tighten up any weaknesses. Athletes on occasions make mistakes, so why could the IAAF not admit that laboratories are also run by human beings who are not infallible?

In my view, where there is even a shadow of a doubt on a dope test, the athlete must be the one given the benefit for their own protection. Instead, as things stand, the athlete is condemned as guilty even when they can prove (as I did) that important mistakes have been made. How was it that the regulations could allow a sample with a pH level close to 9 to be tested when, by all expert agreement, it should have been immediately thrown in the bin? It takes only one such error in a science like drug testing and the result is the devastation of an innocent athlete's life and career.

The IAAF reacted to the ruling of BAF's appeal panel with predictable but infuriating scepticism. Calling the decision 'odd, unusual and surprising', they announced on 31 July that they wanted to refer my case to their own arbitration panel for a decision, 'final and binding to both parties'. If there was anything odd and surprising it was a world sports governing body ruling about my case before they even had the relevant information. The transcripts of the appeal hearing had not even been released when the IAAF made their decision, nor had they seen all the documentation of Simon Gaskell's research. It was hard to believe I would get a fair hearing from an arbitration panel convened by a body which had publicly criticised me from the start. Instead we called for a conference of experts to meet from both sides and consider the Gaskell evidence.

The arguments over the implications of 'The Modahl Affair' for athletics will go on for a long time, but where does it leave the person who has fought and suffered behind the headlines? I have always protested my innocence, the BAF have accepted my innocence, but my story doesn't have the sort of happy ending you get in films with all the loose ends neatly tied. Time can never be reversed. People have asked whether Diane Modahl will ever run again but it isn't simply a matter of pulling on a pair of spikes once more. I was banned from 18 June 1994: the year that followed, in which I battled to clear my name, can never be added to the end of my career. Even if the IAAF finally accept the ruling of the BAF appeal panel, as I believe they must, there is a whole process of mental and physical rehabilitation that has to take place before I could ever set foot on a running track again.

For Vicente and me it has been a formidable test of our resolve, our endurance and our marriage. It has also been a test of faith where I have come out on the other side bruised but strengthened in my belief that God does not abandon those who turn to him in anguish when they are unjustly accused.

Throughout my whole ordeal there were many times I felt I touched rock bottom, but during the appeal I perhaps reached my lowest ebb, where all will to live seemed to desert me. I sat at the back of that room listening to learned voices discussing my case as if it had nothing whatsoever to do with me. Yet there was another life present which was not ready to give up. Repeatedly, during the two days of the appeal, the baby inside me kicked and moved as if it was trying to tell me, '*I want to live*'.

The past wanted to suck me down into the darkness of suicidal despair but the baby called to me insistently from the future. I have suffered a nightmare of such dark depths that it has sometimes threatened to overwhelm me, but with my husband's undying support I have faced it, fought it and outlasted it. The morning after my name was cleared by the appeal panel was like a new day dawning. There may still be plenty of clouds on the horizon but I have found the strength to believe again in a future for myself, for Vicente and for our child – I hope I can run to meet it.

Appendix

Diane's Career Record 1984 to 1994
(major races only)

1984

14/1; MANCHESTER SCHOOLS CH.S.-CROSS-COUNTRY   WINNER
4/2; EUROPEAN CUP-CROSS-COUNTRY FOR TEAMS (SALE H)   3RD TEAM

Date	Competition/Place	Distance	Time	Position
12/5;	WOMEN'S UK LEAGUE-NOTTINGHAM	800M	2,09,8	1ST
		400M	57,0	1ST
22/5;	MANCHESTER SCHOOLS TRACK CH.S.	800M	2,15,2	1ST
2/6;	NORTHERN WAAA CH.S.	800M	2,05,4	1ST
6/6;	OLYMPIC TRIALS IN LONDON	800M	2,03,75	5TH
9/6;	GREATER MANCH. TRACK CH.S.	800M	2,10,9	1ST
16/6;	WAAA BRITISH CH.S.-LONDON	800M	2,04,50	6TH
7/7;	WOMEN'S UK LEAGUE-EDINBURGH	800M	2,05,1	1ST
		400M	55,38	1ST
14/7;	ENGLISH SCHOOLS CH.S.	800M	2,05,7	1ST
29/7;	NORWAY VS ENGLAND IN NORWAY	800M	2,07,03	1ST
4/8;	BELL'S JUNIOR INTERNATIONAL	800M	2,07,06	1ST
26/8;	JUNIOR INTERN.-SEOUL/S.KOREA	800M	2,05,7	1ST
9/9;	BRITISH JUNIOR WAAA CH.S.	400M	55,9	1ST
16/9;	YUGOSLAVIA VS GB–YUGOSLAVIA	800M	2,02,75	5TH

1985

18/5;	GR.MANCH.CH.S.	400M	56,8	1ST
		800M	2,07,4	1ST
16/6;	COVENTRY INVITATIONAL	600M	1,28,4	2ND
21/6;	ENGLAND VS USA	1000M	2,47	3RD
26/6;	BISLETT GAMES-OSLO NORWAY	800M	2,06,0	
29/7;	INVITATIONAL LARVIK-NORWAY	800M	2,03,4	3RD
6/7;	EAST GERMANY VS GB & NI	800M	2,02,76	3RD
27/7;	BRITISH WAAA CH.S.	800M	2,04,50	5TH
24/8;	UK LEAGUE DIV 1	800M	2,05,1	1ST
14/9;	ROMANIA VS ENGLAND IN LONDON	800M	2,02,00	3RD

5/10; NORTHERN CROSS C.CH.S.   1ST

1986

10/5;	UK LEAGUE	800M	2,06,7	1ST
7/6;	BRITISH WAAA CH.S.	800M	2,04,2	1ST

28 TO 31   JULY COMMONWEALTH GAMES IN EDINBURGH
31/7;	FINAL	800M	2,01,12	2ND
10/8;	GRE-SEMI-FINAL	400M	54,7	1ST

26 AND 27   AUGUST EUROPEAN CH.S. STUTTGART GERMANY
26/8;	HEAT	800M	2,03,79	1ST
27/8;	SEMI-FINAL	800M	2,00,84	6TH

30/11; GR.MANCH.CROSS C.CH.S.   WINNER

1987

7/5;	HEAOPOL GAMES IN ISRAEL	800M	2,01,36	1ST
		4×400M		1ST
16/5;	GR.MANCH. CH.S. TRACK	400M	55,0	1ST
25/5;	UK CH.S.	800M	2,01	1ST
13/6;	GB VS POLAND VS CANADA	800M	2,01,7	1ST
4/7;	BISLETT GAMES OSLO NORWAY	800M	1,59,30	4TH
25/7;	BRITISH WAAA CH.S.	800M		1ST
2/8;	GRE SEMI-FINAL	400M	53,5	1ST
14/8;	MILLER LITE INVITATIONAL	800M	2,00,41	1ST
16/8;	GRE FINAL	400M	53,52	1ST
22/8;	BRITISH RECORD	600M	1,26,18	1ST

WORLD CHAMPIONSHIP IN ROME, ITALY
29/8;	HEAT	800M	2,02,57	3RD
30/8;	SEMI-FINAL	800M	1,59,34	6TH

1988

27/6;	BELFAST GAMES	800M	2,02,57	1ST
10/7;	NICE GP FRANCE	800M	1,59,78	1ST
16/7;	GATESHEAD INVITATIONAL	1000M	2,37,00	1ST
31/7;	GRE SEMI-FINAL	400M	54,0	1ST
20/8;	GRE FINAL	400M	54,31	1ST

OLYMPIC GAMES IN SEOUL, S.KOREA
24/9;	HEAT	800M	2,01,79	2ND
25/9;	SEMI-FINAL	800M	1,59,66	4TH
26/9;	FINAL	800M	2,00,77	8TH

8/10;	EIGHT NATIONS IN TOKYO JAPAN	800M	1,59,66	2ND

1989

24/6;	UK LEAGUE	800M	2,02,64	1ST
		1500M	4,20,1	1ST
		1500M	4,20,1	1ST
8/7;	ENGLAND VS CUBA VS BELGIUM	800M	2,02,64	1ST
		1500M	4,12,77	1ST
17/7;	BELFAST INVITATION	800M	2,00,42	1ST
23/7;	UK LEAGUE	400M	54,91	1ST
5/8;	EUROPEAN CUP	800M	2,01,03	5TH
11/8;	BRITISH WAAA CH.S.	800M	2,01,24	1ST
16/8;	ZURICH GP	800M	1,59,99	3RD
18/8;	BERLIN GP	800M	1,59,71	2ND
26/8;	UK LEAGUE	400M	53,9	1ST
28/8;	ENGLAND VS ITALY VS AUSTRALIA	800M	1,59,78	1ST
1/9;	MONTE CARLO GP	800M	2,00,83	3RD
15/9;	LONDON GP	800M	2,00,20	2ND
11/11;	NORTHERN CROSS CH.S.		2ND	

1990

8/1;	INVITATIONAL MANCHESTER	800M	2,02,4	1ST
22/1;	INVITATIONAL NEW ZEALAND	600M	1,26,6	2ND

COMMONWEALTH GAMES IN AUCKLAND NEW ZEALAND

29/1;	HEAT	800M	2,04,86	3RD
1/2;	FINAL COMMONWEALTH CHAMPION	800M	2,00,25	1ST
2/6;	UK CLOSED CH.S. HEAT	400M	53,97	1ST
	FINAL	400M	54,32	1ST
7/7;	UK LEAGUE	800M	2,03,7	1ST
		400M	54,4	1ST
14/7;	BISLETT GAMES OSLO NORWAY	800M	1,58,65	4TH
	ENGLISH RECORD			
16/7;	BELFAST GAMES	800M	2,01,95	3RD
20/7;	LONDON GP	800M	2,00,60	3RD
15/8;	ZURICH GP	800M	1,58,93	7TH

EUROPEAN CHAMPIONSHIP-SPLIT/YUGOSLAVIA

27/8;	HEAT	800M	2,01,65	3RD
28/8;	SEMI-FINAL	800M	2,00,17	5TH
29/8;	FINAL	800M	2,02,62	8TH
9/9;	RIETI ITALY	800M	2,00,33	2ND

1991

16/6;	NORTHERN CH.S.	800M	2,06,51	1ST
7/7;	GRE SEMI-FINAL-LONDON	800M	2,04,98	1ST
		400M	55,12	1ST
19/7;	GB VS USSR-EDINBURGH	800M	2,02,27	4TH
26/7;	BRITISH WAAA CH. S.-B. HAM HEAT	800M	2,04,70	1ST
	FINAL	800M	2,05,19	6TH
4/8;	USSR VS ENGLAND-RUSSIA	800M	2,01,74	1ST

24/8;	UK LEAGUE-COPTHALL	800M	2,05,0	1ST
		400M	53,9	1ST
6/9;	RIETI ITALY	800M	2,00,61	3RD
11/9;	KOBLENZ-GERMANY	800M	2,01,13	1ST
19/10;	5TH AVENUE MILE NEW YORK-USA	MILE	4,39,89	6TH

1992

26/1;	SCOTTISH CH.S.INDOORS	1500M	4,20,2	1ST
5/2;	DN GAMES STOCKHOLM INDOORS	1500M	4,13,52	3RD
23/2;	TSB INV. B.HAM INDOORS	800M	2,02,12	2ND
14/3;	NAT.CROSS C. CH. S. RELAYS		WINNING TEAM	
8/4;	OPEN MEETING MANCH.	800M	2,03,2	1ST
2/5;	MEXICO CITY	400M	53,28	1ST
20/5;	OPEN MEETING MANCH.	800M	2,01,7	1ST
24/5;	NEW YORK GAMES GP	MILE	4,35,32	5TH
1/6;	BRATISLAVA GP	800M	2,00,63	3RD
28/6;	BRITISH WAAA CH. S.	800M	2,00,42	1ST
4/7;	BISLETT GAMES OSLO NORWAY	800M	2,00,46	6TH

OLYMPIC GAMES IN BARCELONA SPAIN

| 31/7; | HEAT | 800M | 2,00,39 | 3RD |
| 1/8; | SEMI-FINAL | 800M | 2,04,32 | 7TH |

| 20/8; | ZURICH GP | 800M | 1,59,96 | 3RD |

1993

9/1;	B.HAM GAMES INDOORS	1500M	4,26,06	1ST
30/1;	GB VS RUSSIA-GLASGOW INDOORS	800M	2,03,35	3RD
9/2;	DN GLOBEN-STOCKHOLM INDOORS	1500M	4,14,59	3RD
13/2;	GB VS USA-B.HAM INDOORS	800M	2,05,15	1ST
20/2;	TSB INVIT.B.HAM INDOORS	800M	2,03,08	1ST
17/5;	OPEN MEETING MANCH.	800M	2,03,9	1ST
22/5;	NEW YORK GAMES GP	800M	1,59,17	4TH
9/6;	ROME GP	800M	1,59,58	4TH
13/6;	UK CH.SHIP -SHEFFIELD	400M	53,38	2ND
20/6;	HENGELO GP-HOLLAND	800M	2,00,62	4TH
26/6;	EUROPA CUP ROME	800M	1,59,7	5TH*

*TIME APX.TIMING SYSTEM FAILED

| 1/8; | GRE SEMI-FINAL | 400M | 54,6 | 1ST |
| 4/8; | ZURICH GP | 800M | 1,59,00 | 7TH |

WORLD CHAMPIONSHIP STUTTGART GERMANY

14/8;	HEAT	800M	2,00,80	1ST
15/8;	SEMI-FINAL	800M	1,59,12	3RD
17/8;	FINAL	800M	1,59,42	4TH

| 26/8; | BERLIN GP | 800M | 2,00,35 | 4TH |
| 29/8; | SHEFFIELD INVITATIONAL | 1000M | 2,35,80 | 2ND |

1994

| 8/3; | DN GAMES STOCKHOLM INDOORS | 800M | 2,02,62 | 3RD |
| 7/5; | UK LEAGUE GRANGEMOUTH | | | |

	/SCOTLAND	800M	2,05,0	1ST
14/5;	GR.MANCH CH.SHIP	800M	2,05,5	1ST
18/5;	OPEN MEETING MANCH.	800M	2,03,7	1ST
4/6;	HENGELO GP HOLLAND	800M	2,01,13	4TH
12/6;	BRITISH AAA CH.SHIP SHEFFIELD	800M	2,01,35	1ST
18/6;	SAN ANTONIO MEETING LISBON/POR.	800M	2,00,50	2ND*

*THE RACE WHERE DIANE WAS TESTED BY THE LISBON LAB.

25/6;	EUROPA CUP WINNER IN B.HAM	800M	2,02,81	1ST
8/7;	LILLE GP-FRANCE	800M	2,00,84	3RD
15/7;	LONDON GP	800M	2,00,50	3RD
29/7;	GOODVILLE GAMES CH.S.	800M	1,59,85	4TH
	ST PETERSBURG-RUSSIA			

EUROPEAN CHAMPIONSHIP HELSINKI-FINLAND

7/8;	HEAT	800M	2,04,46	3RD
8/8;	SEMI-FINAL	800M	2,02,18	6TH

19/8;	OPEN MEETING IN VICTORIA-CANADA	400M	53,5	2ND

COMMONWEALTH GAMES VICTORIA-CANADA

24/8;	SEMI-FINAL	WITHDRAWN

18 TIMES UNDER 2 MINUTES FOR 800M